PRAYING FOR ISRAEL

40 Prayer Ideas a

Penny Valentine

A *Praying God's Word* Resource

Tahilla Press

Eastbourne

ISBN 978-1-907228-07-0

Published by Tahilla Press
e-mail: tahillapress@tahilla.com

DEDICATION

This book is dedicated to all believers in Israel and elsewhere who
are reaching out sacrificially to embrace those on 'the other side',
and so demonstrating the reality and power of the
One New Man in the Kingdom of God.

CONTENTS

FOREWORD

The unremitting strife between Jew and Arab stubbornly seems to resist all human attempts to find a satisfactory resolution. While the present troubles are all too evident, the seeds of mistrust are to be found in past millennia. Even sincere Christians find it hard to be dispassionate observers. Is there any issue on the world agenda that divides the Church more intensely than the Israel/Palestinian conflict?

And yet we as believers are called to be active in the ministry of reconciliation, and to seek to view both these people groups with the compassion and understanding that the Bible reveals lies in the heart of God, who placed them in this strategic part of the world. It is a challenge that we all must face. Penny Valentine has done us a service in helping us to travel this path.

In this short book there is a rich store of material. First there are the succinct studies of various passages from both Old and New Testament that are treated with clarity and perception and give some fresh insights on the Scriptures. The author's purpose however is to use these studies as stimulation for prayer. In this way she follows on from her previous book that many have found helpful, *Praying for the Peace of Jerusalem*. Penny's unjudging embrace of all the nations of the Middle East shines through, as we are encouraged to pray equally for Jews as for Arabs, interceding that the one New Man of Ephesians 2 might become a reality.

The struggle to find a viable 'peace process' based on human diplomacy may seem elusive; all the more reason therefore to focus on God's plan. Penny helps us to recognise this from the Scriptures and to be reminded that it is only in Jesus that the peace that passes all understanding is to be found.

Having spent several years in the Middle East she knows the cost of exercising a genuine love for all people, but by God's grace she shows it can be done. In these pages she indicates how we can become a part of that vision and acquire tools for effective prayer to that end.

Penny and her husband Rod were members of Christ Church, Jerusalem, when I was Rector there. As one who spent a number of years living and serving in the Middle East myself, I count it a privilege to be asked to write this Foreword and I have no hesitation in warmly recommending this book to a wide readership.

May you enjoy these studies, and be encouraged in your resolve to pray with a deeper understanding.

Ray Lockhart
Bath

January 2010

ACKNOWLEDGMENTS

I would like to thank all who have prayed for me as I have written this book; friends near and far, old and new, and including many of the readers of *Praying for the Peace of Jerusalem* who, like Oliver Twist, asked for more! I am especially grateful to our friends Fiona Lindsay who provided so much initial encouragement and did a great job of editing each study as the work progressed, and Derek White for his helpful suggestions and insights, especially about the place of the Arabs in God's salvation plan. In this regard, I am also indebted to Dr Tony Maalouf's excellent book, *Arabs in the Shadow of Israel*, which provided a sound theological base for my research into biblical references to the Arab nations.

Dr. Dwight and Keren Pryor of the Center for Judaic-Christian Studies in Ohio have taught me most of what I know about the Hebrew language and the Hebraic roots of Christianity, and I greatly value their friendship, as well as their teaching. Rev. Ray Lockhart and his wife Jill were a catalyst for our involvement in reconciliation work, as well as being much-appreciated pastors and friends ever since we joined the congregation of Christ Church in Jerusalem many years ago. Those from whom I have learned about God's purposes for Israel over the years are too numerous to mention, but I thank God for them all.

My beloved husband Rod has not only willingly shouldered extra household chores over many months to free me to write, he has had to bear the burden of my occasional writer's block, frequent discouragement and sometimes downright rebellion in the relentless march towards the deadline! As well as helping keep my fingers to the keyboard, he was also my first and most perceptive critic and sounding board for each study. In a very real sense, he shares the credit for this work.

Penny Valentine
January 2010

INTRODUCTION

A wise ministry leader in the Middle East once told me that every Christian called to live and serve in Israel should spend time first in an Arab nation, and likewise, the other way around! In the emotive, polarised climate of the Arab-Israeli conflict it is essential that we stand apart from accepted cultural attitudes on both sides and learn to love both peoples as those who are dear to God's heart.

My husband and I happened to be living in Cairo when God called us to Jerusalem to serve with Christian Friends of Israel, a ministry that expresses unconditional love to the Jewish people in the name of Jesus. We had already learned to love the Arabs, when the Lord overwhelmed us with His heart for His ancient covenant people. Our fifteen years' service with CFI – in Africa and the UK as well as Israel – taught us so much about God's covenant love, His prophetic purposes for Israel and about the Hebraic background to our Bible and to Jesus' teaching. We made many Jewish and Arab friends as we worshipped in a mixed congregation, lived at different times in Jewish and Arab areas, and worked with Messianic and Arab fellowships in various places around the country. What a privilege!

After we finally left Israel to settle back in Britain, I wrote my first study and prayer guide, *Praying for the Peace of Jerusalem,* to help people pray according to the Lord's prophetic purposes as revealed in His Word. It proved helpful to many, in small group contexts as well as for individual devotions. This companion volume now widens the scope to include prayer for Israel's Arab neighbours, also mentioned in the Bible and sharing a prophetic destiny in God's Kingdom. To avoid repetition, I have used different Bible passages in almost every case, and introduced many new issues for prayer. This has meant omitting a number of foundational teachings and important prayer topics found in the first book, and so I strongly encourage readers to use both volumes together in their ongoing prayers.

I have defined the Arab nations quite broadly to include Iran and Turkey who though Muslim, are not ethnically Arab and do not speak Arabic, but whose lands are mentioned in Scripture in connection with the people of Israel. Similarly the nations of Iraq,

Syria, Lebanon and Egypt all speak Arabic and have a broadly Arab culture, although their populations, with sizeable Christian and other minorities, are neither entirely Islamic or entirely Arab in an ethnic sense. As the recent history of Middle Eastern nations may not be familiar to all readers, I have included some historical background in some of the studies.

Throughout, I have used the word 'believers' to indicate those with a living faith in Jesus the Messiah, whether they are from a Jewish, Muslim, traditional Arab Christian or expatriate background. In general, Jewish believers are known as 'Messianic', rather than 'Christian' – it means the same thing, without the negative connotations that the word 'Christian' carries in the Jewish culture. All Hebrew or Arabic words, other than anglicised forms of them, are shown in italics. Unless otherwise indicated, all Bible quotations are from the English Standard Version.

It is my fervent prayer that this book will help many Christian friends of Israel to receive God's heart of love for the Arab peoples, alongside their love and commitment to the Jews. Likewise may those whom God has called to minister to the Arab world, learn to pray with God's heart for the people of Israel. These are back in their homeland and amongst their Arab brethren by God's power and promise in fulfilment of His Word, and are a key to the salvation of the Muslim world. After all, Jews and Arabs of the Middle East, as the prophet Isaiah says (19:24), are called together to be *'a blessing in the midst of the earth'*. For that reason, this book begins with a study on reconciliation, though the rest are in biblical order.

Penny Valentine
pennyprayer@googlemail.com

'In that day Israel will be the third with Egypt and Assyria, a blessing in the midst of the earth, whom the LORD of hosts has blessed, saying, "Blessed be Egypt my people, and Assyria the work of my hands, and Israel my inheritance"'
(Isaiah 19:24, 25).

'All this is from God, who through Christ [Messiah] reconciled us to himself and gave us the ministry of reconciliation' (2 Corinthians 5:18).

**Passage for study and prayer:
2 Corinthians 5:1-21**

Reconciliation is all about relationships, and the whole Bible is about reconciliation, from man's first separation from God in the garden, to the New Jerusalem of Revelation, when the face-to-face relationship with Him will finally be restored and God will dwell forever with His people. At the very centre is the Messiah, through whom both Jew and Gentile are reconciled with God, and therefore with each other. The ministry of reconciliation that Paul talks about in this passage is primarily that between man and God through the death and resurrection of Jesus – but Jesus brings reconciliation between people too. In the context of the Middle East, where hatred and fear between Jew and Arab is so deeply entrenched and religiously based, it is only when people become literally a new creation in Him that true and lasting reconciliation is possible.

The Holy Spirit enables believers to walk by faith not by sight, to be controlled by the love of Jesus, to regard no one according to the flesh, and to be ambassadors for God's Kingdom, proving to 'the other side' that in His Kingdom there really can be true unity and love.

And this is actually happening! Imagine the scene – an Israeli hospital where two seriously ill men lie side by side in Intensive Care. (By the way, who said that Israel was an apartheid state?) One is a Jewish Zionist who has spent a lifetime in Messiah's service, and the other is a Hamas fighter, critically injured by gunmen from the rival Fatah group, and airlifted in from the West Bank by the Israeli Air Force. Beside them are the Jewish man's wife, and the Palestinian's brother. The older woman reaches out, with her few words of Arabic and the love of Jesus, to this terrified and hostile young man who has so suddenly found himself 'in enemy territory'. After her husband dies a few weeks later, the young man insists on meeting and embracing her – and today, several years later, this 'mother in Israel' and her 'Palestinian son' and his family are still in close contact. When terrorist rockets hit her town one day, his urgent phone call to check on her welfare meant more than any other! His view of Jews and Israelis (and Jesus) is totally changed. Arab believers have embraced him too. Her ministry has expanded over the 'green line' to include other relationships with Palestinians, both Christian and Muslim, who alike are deeply impacted by the love and interest of a Jewish Israeli. This ongoing story, and others like it, is a beacon of hope in the bleak landscape of the Israeli-Palestinian conflict.

 Pray the Word

Praise God for the power of true reconciliation! Pray for many more Israeli believers to take risks and reach out in the power of the Holy Spirit into 'enemy territory' no matter what it costs, and to know His provision and protection. *'He who has prepared us for this very thing is God, who has given us the Spirit as a guarantee. So we are always of good courage'* (vv5, 6).

Pray for great blessing upon the Arab and Jewish believers who are already committed to walk this path. As they challenge negative stereotypes, pray that their example will have a powerful impact on all around them, bringing change to attitudes and behaviour. *'For the love of Christ controls us…From now on, therefore, we regard no one according to the flesh'* (vv14, 16).

Praise God for this former Hamas sympathiser and others like him, whose lives are being changed forever by the ministry of reconciliation! *'Therefore, if anyone is in Christ, he is a new creation. The old has passed away; behold, the new has come'* (v17). Pray for their witness, and that many more will forsake hatred and violence for a new and better way in the Messiah.

'The LORD said to Abram, after Lot had separated from him, "Lift up your eyes and look from the place where you are, northward and southward and eastward and westward,
for all the land that you see I will give to you and to your offspring forever"' (Genesis 13:14, 15).

 Passage for study and prayer: Genesis 13:1-18

Abram was a nomad – living in tents, moving from place to place to ensure grazing for his flocks and herds, dependent on seasons and weather for sufficient water. Over the years, even though he made mistakes, God's promised blessing brought him prosperity – and it created a problem. His nephew Lot was also growing richer and the land could no longer support them both, let alone the other tribes living amongst them. Their servants were quarrelling and the family discord obviously grieved Abram. He proposed a solution: they must separate, and he gives Lot the choice. Lot decided on the fertile Jordan plain, complete with cities including the notoriously sinful Sodom, and Abram stayed in the hills of Canaan, where he had already built altars to the Lord at Shechem (Nablus today), Bethel and Hebron.

Abram's lot, though not his own choice necessarily, was indeed the inheritance God had chosen for him. The Lord affirmed His previous promise given in Genesis 12:7, of this particular patch of territory, but this time, He adds two important words – in Hebrew, 'ad olam'. This literally means 'as far as the vanishing point' or 'until eternity', i.e. forever. The dimension of time is added to that of space! It is hard to escape the absoluteness of this phrase; forever is forever is forever.

Then He adds something else – Abram's descendants will be as numerous as the dust of the earth. Just as eternity cannot be ended, so his descendants cannot be numbered, and forever they will know that they have a special inheritance in this particular small patch of land at the crossroads of the continents. Today these hills are known to Israeli Jews as Judea and Samaria, and to everyone else as the West Bank or Occupied Territories. Together with Jerusalem, they are at the heart of the Arab-Israeli conflict, and it is easy to see why. Both Jews and Arabs claim the right to live in the area, as indeed they both did for centuries, until all Jews were expelled in 1948. Having returned since 1967, many find it unthinkable to leave their 'forever inheritance' again.

 Pray the Word

Praise the LORD that once again there are Jews worshipping Him in the places where their forefather Abram built altars to the LORD, as testimony to His grace and the truth of His Word. *'Arise, walk through the length and the breadth of the land, for I will give it to you'* (v17). Pray that established Jewish communities will not have to be uprooted again from their inheritance.

Pray fervently also that they may have the same spirit as Abram, not desiring strife with their Arab brothers, but to live in peace and blessing. *'Let there be no strife between you and me, and between your herdsmen and my herdsmen, for we are kinsmen'* (v8). Pray the same prayer for their Arab neighbours, and pray for mutually beneficial, rather than destructive, relationships between the communities.

Stand in prayer against the religious spirits on both sides that radicalise the conflict and work against God's purposes to make Israel a blessing to its neighbours. Pray for the Kingdom and rule of God to come through faith in the Messiah, to both Jew and Arab. *'Your Kingdom come, your will be done...'* (Matthew 6:10).

17

'Behold, you are pregnant and shall bear a son. You shall call his name Ishmael, because the LORD has listened to your affliction. He shall be a wild donkey of a man, his hand against everyone and everyone's hand against him, and he shall dwell over against all his kinsmen' (Genesis 16:11b, 12).

 Passage for study and prayer: Genesis 16:1-16

Ishmael is one of the foremost ancestors of the Arab peoples. Some Christians teach that he was conceived because of Abram and Sarai's lack of faith, making his birth a costly mistake that has led to all today's conflicts in the Middle East! But this passage clearly proves otherwise. Sarai accepted that the Lord had caused her barrenness (v2), and God's promise had not specified her as the mother of the promised son (see Genesis 15:4). So as was normal custom at the time, she offered her Egyptian maid to Abram as a second wife and surrogate mother, through whom perhaps God would give the promised heir. Unfortunately, pregnant Hagar took advantage of her new social status to belittle her mistress (v4), who was furious and with Abram's permission treated her slave harshly to reassert her authority (v6). Hagar ran away from this persecution into the wilderness, where in her rejection and desperation, she had an encounter with God.

God is sovereign, so He could easily have closed Hagar's womb too, but He didn't. Instead He revealed Himself personally to Hagar in the midst of her crisis. Far from rejecting her, he reassured her that the child she carried would also inherit the promise of descendants beyond numbering (vv9, 10). Ishmael was the first of only four children in the Bible to be directly named by God or angelic messenger (the others were Isaac, John the Baptist and Jesus). Meaning 'God hears', his name was an assurance of the Lord's love for him and his mother (v11). This son of a slave would grow up to be a *pere adam*, 'a wild donkey of a man', as free as the wild donkey (*pere*) so beautifully described in Job 39:5-8. Fiercely independent, he would live untamed in the deserts alongside his brothers (v12). Hagar was comforted, and realising that she had met with God Himself, she became the only person in Scripture to give Him a name – *El Roi*, 'the God who sees'. In the strength of this new understanding she was able to obey His command to return and submit to her mistress, so that her son could grow up in his father's godly home.

 Pray the Word

Thank God that the Arab peoples are not a mistake, but those whom He loves and blesses, living in the Middle East alongside His covenant people by His design and plan. '*...he shall dwell over against all his kinsmen*' (v12). Pray that Arab states will recognize Israel's right to be a nation in their midst and sincerely desire to be at peace with them, and that Israelis will reciprocate.

Pray for Arab women who are often cruelly treated in their homes, to encounter the Lord as Hagar did. *"You are a God of seeing," for she said, "Truly here I have seen him who looks after me"'* (v13). Give thanks for those beaming the message of God's love into homes via radio and television, and pray for much fruit. Pray too for Israeli victims of domestic violence.

Pray for a great revelation of Biblical truth across the Arab world, that will bring them into their destiny in God's Kingdom. Arabs are made by God to be free, but so many are in bondage to a false religion. '*You will know the truth, and the truth will set you free...So if the Son sets you free, you will be free indeed*' (John 8:32, 36).

LAUGHTER AND PAIN

'And Sarah said, "God has made laughter for me; everyone who hears will laugh over me"' (Genesis 21:6).

 Passage for study and prayer: Genesis 21:1-21

The birth of Isaac was such a laughing matter! Both Abraham (see Genesis 17:17) and Sarah (Genesis 18:12) had laughed in utter disbelief when they were told that the Lord would give them a son – after all, Abraham was 99 years old and Sarah was 90, and their bodies were worn out! It seemed totally impossible, but nothing is too difficult for the Lord, as He pointed out (Genesis 18:14). Sure enough, Sarah conceived and at the appointed time Isaac, whose name means 'laughter', was born. This laughter, made by God, was pure joy. We feel Sarah's joy after a lifetime of disappointment, Abraham's joy at knowing the Lord's faithfulness, God's joy in revealing His creative power and perfect plan for blessing. The fulfilment of God's perfect plan always brings joy, and daily as these parents enjoyed their son, his name reminded them both of their unbelief, and God's grace and glory. Hallelujah!!

When Isaac was safely weaned at about 3 years old, it was cause for a huge party! Again there was laughter, this time Ishmael's as he played with his little brother. (Some translations say that Ishmael was mocking or teasing Isaac but the Hebrew does not actually imply this). Sarah noticed, and suddenly realised what a threat big brother Ishmael could be to Isaac's inheritance in the future. At once she demanded that Abraham cast out the bondwoman and her son to avoid any possible future conflict.

Abraham, who deeply loved Ishmael, was horrified – but then God Himself endorsed Sarah's understanding of the issues at stake. He reminded Abraham that this miracle son was His appointed legal heir to the covenant promises (look at Genesis 17:18, 19). The Lord would care for and bless Ishmael too, as He had promised, but there had to be a separation. However unfair it may seem to our modern humanistic mindset, Abraham's descendants through Isaac had to be set apart for the sake of God's salvation purposes, even though this brought pain alongside joy and laughter.

 Pray the Word

Declare God's sovereign power to accomplish His purposes His way, and rejoice with His people, today back in their land and their holy city after centuries of exile, just as He promised. Stand in prayer against those who would deny Israel's right to its ancient homeland, and pray for the fulfilment of all God's perfect plans for the restoration of Israel. *'But be glad and rejoice forever in that which I create; for behold, I create Jerusalem to be a joy, and her people to be a gladness'* (Isaiah 65:18).

Pray for those in Palestinian refugee camps, displaced in Israel's 1948 war of independence and not yet fully absorbed, for political reasons, by any Arab nation. Pray especially for the younger generations, nurtured on handouts and hatred of Israel, to be set free by God's Spirit to come into the fullness of His Kingdom blessing. *'Fear not, for God has heard the voice of the boy where he is. And God was with the boy, and he grew up'* (vv17, 20).

Pray for a mighty revelation of His presence and love to destroy the spirit of rejection in the Arab heart, and open them to hear and respond to His word. *'...the LORD has listened to your affliction'* (Genesis 16:11). Ishmael's banishment sowed seeds of rejection in the Arab psyche that are still recognized as a problem today, especially colouring attitudes to the Jews and to the good news of Jesus.

Pray for all ministering His love in person or via the airwaves in the Arab nations.

THE BINDING OF ISAAC

*'I will surely bless you, and I will surely multiply
your offspring as the stars of heaven and as the
sand that is on the seashore. And your offspring
shall possess the gate of his enemies, and in your
offspring shall all the nations of the earth be
blessed, because you have obeyed My voice'*
(Genesis 22:17, 18).

 Passage for study and prayer: Genesis 22:1-19

This was Abraham's greatest test. He had already lost one son, sent
away as a teenager years before, so that he would not compete with
Isaac, the son of the promise. Now God seemed to be asking the
unthinkable – that he should offer Isaac as a sacrifice on Mount
Moriah, a very specific place. Why? It seems horrific that the Lord
would even want such a thing, yet Abraham obeyed without
question. He must have been very sure he heard from God.

It was a three-day journey – plenty of time to reconsider while on
the road, but when Abraham arrived near the appointed place, he
left behind the servants and donkey, and went on alone with Isaac,
to worship (v5). The word describing Isaac in this verse shows that
he was no longer a child, but a youth, able to carry the wood laid
across his shoulders (v6 - does this remind you of anything, by the
way?). He asked where the lamb was, and Abraham by faith
declared that the Lord would provide – and indeed, at the very last
minute, He did! The ram with its head caught in the thicket of
thorns replaced the unresisting Isaac on the altar, and Abraham
passed the test (v12). What a relationship Abraham had with God -
and then what about Isaac? He trusted his father totally and was
obedient in turn to his will.

A faithful, obedient father, a beloved and willing son, a lamb for a
sacrifice, a journey to a specific hilltop in a particular part of the
promised land, as clearly guided by God. What a picture! This
passage lays the foundation for the focal point of God's entire plan

of redemption in the Messiah, as revealed throughout the Bible. No wonder the Lord declares that the promised blessings of the Abrahamic covenant, both for his descendants and for the nations of the entire world, have been finally secured by Abraham's sacrificial obedience to His Word (v18). In Judaism, this important passage is called the *Akedah,* or 'Binding', and raises many thorny theological questions for those who study it.

 Pray the Word

Pray that as they study this portion of Scripture, today's children of Abraham may receive revelation of its fullest meaning through the Holy Spirit. *'Abraham said, "God will provide for Himself the lamb for a burnt offering, my son." So they went both of them together'* (v8).

Mount Moriah is traditionally identified with the Temple Mount in the heart of Jerusalem, and as a holy site to both Jews and Muslims, it is at the heart of the Middle East conflict too. Muslims believe that Ishmael, not Isaac, was offered up where the Dome of the Rock now stands.

Pray for the Holy Spirit to supernaturally reveal to Muslims how God has provided for them in Jesus, as they worship there. *'And Abraham called the name of the place, The-Lord-Will Provide; as it is said to this day, In the mount of the LORD it will be provided'* (v14).

Give thanks for many today who are serving Him in costly obedience in the nations of the Middle East. Great blessing follows obedience in the purposes of God. Pray for the gifts of faith and faithfulness, and for much blessing on their ministries. *'By myself I have sworn, says the LORD, because you have done this thing, and have not withheld... I will bless you,'* (vv16, 17).

BLESSING BRINGS TROUBLE!

'Then Isaac sowed in that land, and reaped in the same year a hundredfold; and the LORD blessed him. The man began to prosper, and continued prospering until he became very prosperous ... So the Philistines envied him' (Genesis 26:12-14, NKJV).

 Passage for study and prayer: Genesis 26:1-33

Have you ever wondered why people hate the Jews? Anti-Semitism (unreasoning hatred of Jews) has accompanied the people of Israel throughout history, and this passage helps us understand why. For a start, the Lord often puts His covenant people into difficult situations where they are forced into an encounter with Him – see vv1, 2 and 24. Isaac's revelations of the LORD in the midst of these trials not only demanded trust and obedience like his father's, but also made sure that the promises made to Abraham, were restated and confirmed to the next generation (vv3-5, 24). Then secondly, God also desires to test the nations, amongst whom He plants His people as a challenge and a witness.

How did the Philistines respond to this challenge? When Isaac allowed his fears to make him lie about Rebekah, Abimelech responded very graciously and gave them his protection (v11). However, when the blessing of God followed, things changed. Jealousy turned to fear of Isaac's growing economic power, and led to his expulsion from their midst (vv14, 16). Then when Isaac tried to open up his father's wells, blocked up after Abraham's death by the Philistines, each was reclaimed as soon as it was functional again. The Philistines didn't want him anywhere near their territory, competing for precious resources! Isaac gave in and tried somewhere else, desperate to avoid conflict and always hoping to live in peace. (How often this has happened down the centuries – does it sound familiar today?)

Finally, back in Beersheba, already an important place of worship and revelation of God, there is an interesting replay of a 'peace process' that first took place between Abimelech and Abraham in Genesis 21. 'Abimelech', meaning 'my father is king', and 'Phicol', were titles rather than names, so these were probably different individuals. The Philistines approached Isaac (who was understandably suspicious given their past record!) because they had recognized Isaac's God (v28). Together they made a covenant that brought reconciliation, and confirmed Beersheva as part of Israel's inheritance.

 Pray the Word

Search your own heart for any shred of anti-Semitism you may have absorbed from your background or culture, and ask the Lord for grace to stand with His people, who bear a heavy price for their calling to be a witness to the nations. *'And Abimelech said to Isaac, "Go away from us, for you are mightier than we are"'* (v16). Pray that all Christians, especially those from Middle Eastern nations, may do the same.

Pray for the Jewish people to be strengthened in the face of hatred and persecution, and look to their God and His Messiah for help. *'Those who hate me without a cause are more than the hairs of my head; they are mighty who would destroy me, being my enemies wrongfully. Though I have stolen nothing, I still must restore it'* (Psalm 69:4, NKJV).

Pray for Israel's neighbours to recognise the Lord's blessing, and to desire to live in peace with His people. Pray for genuine reconciliation in the Middle East. *'We have certainly seen that the LORD is with you. So we said, 'Let there be now an oath between us...'* (v28, NKJV).

BACK WITH HIS BROTHERS

'Now Joseph was governor over the land. He was the one who sold to all the people of the land. And Joseph's brothers came and bowed themselves before him with their faces to the ground' (Genesis 42:6).

 Passage for study and prayer: Genesis 42:1-24

For millennia, Jews have suffered at the hands of 'Christians'. Since the time of the early Church Fathers when enmity between church and synagogue led to a growing breach, and the church grew away from its Hebraic roots to become more and more 'Gentilised', the person of Jesus has been masked to the Jewish eye. Just as his brothers could not recognise the 'Egyptian' Joseph, looking totally foreign and speaking through an interpreter in a language they couldn't understand, so Jews see no connection between the Christian Jesus and their own concept of the Messiah spoken of in their Scriptures. They do not realise that Jesus is as Jewish as they are! Sadly, many Christians do not realise this either, and their understanding of the Scriptures and of Jesus' teaching is greatly impoverished as a result.

Joseph not only knew his own brothers immediately, he also realised as they bowed down before him that the dreams he had had many years before were fulfilled in that moment. God had had a plan through all the years of suffering – He had made him an 'Egyptian' leader not only to save the Egyptians from starvation, but also his own family and tribe. In fact God had an even greater purpose. Joseph was the 'hook' to draw the sons of Israel into Egypt for a season, where they would eventually become suffering slaves, as he had been. This set the stage for the Passover and the great redemption out of Egypt back to the Promised Land, which established Israel as a nation in special relationship with Yahweh and in turn was a shadow of God's greater redemption through Jesus, the Lamb of God.

There are many parallels between Jesus and Joseph. We can be greatly encouraged as we read the rest of the story. Joseph harshly tested his brothers to prove their repentance for their treatment of him, and their care for Benjamin, his beloved little brother; but the ultimate purpose was the reuniting of the whole family. He understood their hearts, and when he finally spoke to them alone in their mother tongue, he revealed himself unmistakeably as their brother (see 45:3).

 Pray the Word

Praise God that Jesus understands and loves His brothers in the flesh even though they do not recognize Him! Pray for them in their time of testing and confusion, when their integrity as a nation is constantly questioned. May it lead them to repent and submit to His authority. *'In truth we are guilty concerning our brother, in that we saw the distress of his soul, when he begged us and we did not listen. That is why this distress has come upon us'* (v21).

Give thanks for growing numbers of Messianic believers in Israel today, who like Benjamin who shared both a father and a mother with Joseph, are brothers of Jesus both in the natural and spiritual! Pray for them to be accepted and respected in Israeli society as true Jews even though they believe Jesus is the Messiah.
'Send...and...bring your brother, while you remain confined, that your words may be tested, whether there is truth in you' (v16).

Pray that the authentic Jewish face of Jesus will appear ever more clearly as many Christians in our day learn more about the Hebrew language and first century Jewish culture within which He lived and ministered. Pray for those studying and teaching these truths, that the church worldwide will be immeasurably strengthened as it reconnects with its Hebraic roots. *'Remember it is not you who support the root, but the root that supports you'* (Romans 11:18).

WHAT IS GOD'S NAME?

'God also said to Moses, "Say this to the people of Israel, 'The LORD [YHWH], the God of your fathers, the God of Abraham, the God of Isaac, and the God of Jacob, has sent me to you.' This is my name forever, and thus I am to be remembered..."'' (Exodus 3:15).

 Passage for study and prayer: Exodus 3:1-22

Does God have a name? A personal name, that is, that only belongs to Him and no other? Many today would say that He has many names - that if you worship the Muslim Allah, or Buddha, or Krishna, you are still worshipping the same God. Muslims believe that Allah is God's unique name, and some forbid Christians to use it. True, it is found in the Arabic Bible, but that is because it is the Arabic word for 'God'; in Hebrew, *'elohim'*. In answer to Moses' specific question about His name, God *(elohim)* says, "I AM WHO I AM" – *'hayah asher hayah'*. He tells Moses to tell the Israelites "I AM has sent you." *Hayah* is the root of the four Hebrew letters *YHWH,* that God says is His name forever.

Out of respect, Jews substitute the word *Adonai* for *YHWH* when reading or praying, and in conversation simply say *HaShem* – the Name. Likewise Bible translators render *YHWH* as LORD or GOD, in capitals, to distinguish it from other terms for God. Meaning the eternal, ever-present one, who was and is and is to come, it is also the covenant name by which God revealed and committed Himself to Abraham, Isaac and Jacob. Many other names revealing aspects of His character incorporate this name, sometimes shortened to 'Yah'.

This revelation of His Name to Moses is crucial, because the whole Bible is about showing who the only true God really is and what He is really like. Everything God does with the people of Israel is for this purpose. The LORD calls Moses because He wants to reveal more of His saving power and faithful covenant love, to the Israelites – and also to their Egyptian oppressors. He intends to redeem Israel supernaturally from suffering and slavery and make them into a nation uniquely associated with Him, in the Land which He promised to their fathers, all so that they in turn may be the bearers of the revelation of His Name and character to others. Moses' obedience (finally!) to the LORD's call means He can use him as part of this ongoing unveiling to the world, of the very nature of the One who is both creator and redeemer of all mankind. The first five foundational books of the Bible, the *'Torah'* or 'teachings', are attributed to Moses, the first great leader of Israel. No wonder the god of this world offers so many counterfeit gods and scriptures to try and deceive – but when one compares them, they cannot possibly be the same!

 Pray the Word

Pray for Israelis seeking truth in other religions or the New Age to have a burning bush experience of the God of their fathers, and return to His Word. Many, especially the young, are looking for the LORD in the wrong places! *'When the LORD saw that he turned aside to see, God called to him out of the bush, "Moses, Moses!" And he said, "Here I am"'* (v4).

Pray for the LORD to use the present dangers Israel faces to bring a fresh revelation of who He is, both to them and to the nations around them. *'And now, behold, the cry of the people of Israel has come to me... Come, I will send you to Pharaoh that you may bring my people, the children of Israel, out of Egypt'* (vv9, 10). Pray for the calling and anointing of key leaders to do His will.

Give thanks for new technology which is making the Bible available in the Arab world via the Internet, mobile phone downloads and satellite broadcasts. Pray for God's Word to do its work of breaking down strongholds of deception and revealing the true God. *'Is not my word like fire, declares the LORD, and like a hammer that breaks the rock in pieces?'* (Jeremiah 23:29).

'And the LORD spoke to Moses in the wilderness of Sinai, in the first month of the second year after they had come out of the land of Egypt, saying, "Let the people of Israel keep the Passover at its appointed time"' (Numbers 9:1, 2).

 Passage for study and prayer: Numbers 9:1-14

Isn't it amazing to think that now in the twenty-first century, many millennia after this very first occasion when the Feast of Passover was celebrated to remember God's great redemption and deliverance from Egypt, it is still kept by the Jewish people at the appointed time each year? Passover, *Pesach* in Hebrew, is the great family festival of freedom that teaches the truths of the Exodus to the next generation. It is the very fulcrum of Jewish faith and identity that has linked the people of Israel together through the centuries. Right from the start, God decreed that nothing was to interfere with it – not even a death causing ritual uncleanness, or travel away from home (v10). Failure to keep it was such sin it would cost one's place as a part of God's people (v13). The statutes and rules of Passover (v3) are laid down in the books of Exodus and Leviticus, and even today unleavened bread and bitter herbs (v11) are still essential elements of the Passover meal, the *seder*. Every part of the ritual enacts the drama of the first Passover night, as laid down in the traditional liturgy, the *Haggadah*, and even the most secular of Jews will make an effort to participate in this annual gathering, and pass on its story to their children.

The blessing of Passover even extended to those outside the house of Israel (v14). Any stranger who happened to be around was welcome to share freely in the celebration! What a wonderful foreshadowing of the redemption offered to all mankind when the blood of Jesus, the ultimate Passover Lamb, was shed at Passover. Within a generation of His final sacrifice the Temple was destroyed and no more Passover lambs could be annually offered. The

Passover liturgy that has evolved since then has some interesting elements. Christians and Messianic Jews see Jesus' death and resurrection clearly portrayed in the ritual of the *afikomen,* or 'dessert'. One of three pieces of *matzot,* unleavened bread which is striped, bruised and pierced in appearance, is taken and broken in two. The larger portion is wrapped in a napkin and hidden, ready to be found later by the children. It is then exchanged for a reward before being shared out amongst everyone and eaten as the final 'dessert' of the meal. A place is always set at table for Elijah, the prophet who will return to herald the Messiah's arrival, and a child is sent to the front door to look for his coming. At Passover the Jews reaffirm their hope that Messiah will come to deliver, just as for centuries they prayed at the end of the *seder* to return to the Promised Land – "Next year, in Jerusalem!"

 Pray the Word

Praise God that year by year, the celebration of Passover reminds Jewish families of His great power and love, and of their hope of final redemption. Pray for the Holy Spirit to use it to stir hearts and bring revelation, especially of the Lamb of God. *'For Christ [Messiah] our Passover lamb, has been sacrificed'* (1 Corinthians 5:7). Pray especially for children to be deeply touched by the message of this season, and for the witness of Messianic believers to family and friends.

Pray that those still in the Diaspora will be convicted to return home as they remember Jerusalem. Today, there are millions keeping the Feast again in Israel after many long centuries of exile. *'If I forget you O Jerusalem, let my right hand forget its skill!'* (Psalm 137:5).

Praise God that He always intended for Gentiles to share in the Passover! *'And if a stranger sojourns among you and would keep the Passover to the LORD, according to the statute of the Passover and according to its rule, so shall he do'* (v14). Pray that the church will rediscover the intimate connection between Passover and Easter, deliberately obscured through centuries of Christian anti-Semitism since the time of the early Church Fathers.

'But the land that you are going over to possess is a land of hills and valleys, which drinks water by the rain from heaven, a land that the LORD your God cares for. The eyes of the LORD your God are always upon it, from the beginning of the year to the end of the year' (Deuteronomy 11:11, 12)

**Passage for study and prayer:
Deuteronomy 11:1-21**

On the doorstep of their destination after 40 years in the wilderness, Moses is preparing the Israelites for their entry into a new life as God's people in the land promised to their forefathers. In this passage he introduces a theme that is echoed throughout their subsequent history and is still very relevant today. Unlike Egypt, where the Nile provides a constant source of water and therefore life (v10), tiny Israel cannot depend on any major river system for a water supply. Its hills and valleys are watered only by seasonal rainfall (v11). This rain from heaven forms streams, or 'wadis', many of which are dry much of the year, and it sinks through the porous rock to replenish the underground aquifers.

The Sea of Galilee, Israel's main fresh water source, is itself dependent on the springs and snowmelt that flow down from the heights of Mount Hermon to form the headwaters of the famous (though not deep and wide!) Jordan River, that then flows out of the lake for only a short distance before being swallowed into the chemical soup of the Dead Sea. Although modern Israel is renowned for its advanced water technology and desert irrigation, it is still totally dependent on rainfall to maintain its water supply.

And that is just what the LORD intended! Rain was a very tangible reminder of His peoples' dependence on Him. In Egypt, they could plant their seeds and water their crops through their own efforts, but now they would have to look to God's grace, all year round. The rain would act as a barometer of their relationship; if they loved and served God as He longed for, the early and latter rains would fall, but if not, He would shut up the heavens. It is interesting that Moses here stresses God's love for the land itself (v11), a mirror for His love of His people. When they reciprocated, the land itself would blossom – but the opposite was equally true. That way, the LORD could get their attention when they sinned or turned from Him.

Rain and repentance are closely linked throughout the Bible, and today is no different. Israel has an ongoing water crisis, as a growing population and modern lifestyles stretch water resources more and more. Underground aquifers are in danger of depletion and contamination, and some small rivers are badly polluted. The Sea of Galilee and the Dead Sea are at record low levels. Water is also a very contentious part of negotiations with the Palestinians and Syrians. Do you think God is trying to say something?

 Pray the Word

Pray for the Holy Spirit to convict of sin and bring repentance whenever Israelis gather to pray for rain, especially during *Succot* (Tabernacles). *'And if you will indeed obey my commandments… to love the LORD your God, and to serve him with all your heart and with all your soul, he will give the rain for your land in its season'* (vv13, 14). Pray for abundance of repentance and rain.

Pray that Israel's water policies may be a source of blessing for the whole region. *'I will make you as a light for the nations'* (Isaiah 49:6). Pray for wise and fair water policies, both domestic and regionally, and for God's blessing on research into desalination, recycling and water conservation.

Praise God for His love and mercy in providing rain for all mankind, and pray that many will look to Him for rain and snow in all the thirsty lands of the Middle East. *'For he makes his sun rise on the evil and on the good, and sends rain on the just and on the unjust'* (Matthew 5:45).

'...for the LORD your God, he is God in the heavens above and on the earth beneath. Now then, please swear to me by the LORD that, as I have dealt kindly with you, you also will deal kindly with my father's house... and deliver our lives from death.'
(Joshua 2:11-13)

 Passage for study and prayer: Joshua 2:1-24

The LORD made a promise to Abraham in Genesis 12:3 that those who blessed him would be blessed. Generations later, as Abraham's descendants stood at the gateway to the Promised Land after their great redemption from slavery in Egypt, Rahab the Jericho prostitute proved that this promise was true. She had realised who the men were that had come to her house, and was very clear about why she hid them, lied about them to the authorities, and helped them to escape. She had heard about the power of their God in redeeming them from Egypt, and destroying their enemies. She realised that He was the true God of both heaven and earth, and it was useless to try and oppose Him. Rather she would choose His side, and hopefully rescue her whole family from inevitable destruction.

She struck a bargain with the spies, that as she had been kind to them, so they would swear to her by the LORD that they would spare her and her family when God gave them the city. They agreed, and thought up a plan, surely inspired by the memory of the night of Passover a generation before. Rahab was to gather all her relatives into her house on the city wall, and tie a red cord in the window as a sign of her trust in God and His people. As long as they remained behind the red cord, they would be safe. She kept her side of the bargain to keep secret the coming attack, and the spies returned home to tell of the terror of the LORD that had fallen upon the people of Jericho. Later, Rahab and her family were indeed rescued by her two friends before the final destruction of the city, and she eventually became part of God's covenant people (Joshua 6:21-25). What's more, she married Salmon and their son was Boaz, so she was a great-great-grandmother of King David, and therefore, a many greats grandmother of Jesus! (Matthew 1:5). Thus Rahab the lowly Gentile prostitute became a very specific part of God's salvation plan for the whole earth, and all because she made that choice - to bless those God had blessed.

 Pray the Word

Praise the Lord that He longs to save and bless those who will bless His people. Ask Him to raise up many in the nations of the Middle East with the heart of Rahab, in spite of the pain of history and constant hostile propaganda. May they may be blessed with the knowledge of the true God and His love for them. *'I will bless those who bless you…'* (Genesis 12:3).

Pray that the fear of the LORD may fall on the enemies constantly threatening Israel's borders who seek her destruction. *'I know that the LORD has given you the land, and that the fear of you has fallen upon us, and that all the inhabitants of the land melt away before you'* (v9).

Today, there are still those in Palestinian areas who risk their own lives to save Israeli lives, and though many are given refuge in Israel, they are not always treated as they deserve.

Pray for protection and blessing for them and their families. Pray that Israel will be mindful of her responsibilities and treat them with fairness and respect. *'If you do not tell this business of ours, then when the LORD gives us the land we will deal kindly and faithfully with you'* (v14).

VIOLENCE BREEDS VIOLENCE

'And God sent an evil spirit between Abimelech and the leaders of Shechem, and [they] dealt treacherously with Abimelech, that the violence done to the seventy sons of Jerubbaal might come, and their blood be laid on Abimelech their brother, who killed them, and on the men of Shechem, who strengthened his hands to kill his brothers' (Judges 9:23, 24)

 Passage for study and prayer: Judges 9:1-57.

This long chapter tells one of the saddest stories in the Bible. It describes what followed the death of Gideon, nicknamed Jerubbaal, Israel's great hero whose success in delivering Israel from its enemies was based on his obedience to God's command to purge the land of idolatry. Abimelech, his son by a female servant, approached his mother's relatives in Shechem (later called Samaria, and today's Nablus). Because he was their kinsman, they and the local leaders decided to help set him up as king. Worship to Baal was back in fashion already in Shechem (vv4, 27), and they gave money from Baal's shrine to hire thugs who helped him murder all his 70 brothers except one. Jotham escaped, and soon challenged the leaders of Shechem with some profound truths.

His parable of the trees (vv 7-15) showed that those who actively seek power for themselves are worthless people with nothing better to do. Further, those who support and submit to them will get what they deserve (vv16-20). If they had acted with integrity and good faith in what they did to Jerubbaal's sons, after he had risked his life to deliver them from Midian, then all would be well – but if not, then fire from Abimelech himself would be the source of their destruction and cause of their downfall.

The rest of the story shows the terrible outworking of Jotham's curse, which interestingly, he uttered from Mount Gerizim, the Mount of Blessing (see Deuteronomy 27:12). Abimelech ruled

Israel for only three years before the bloody violence of his rise to power bore the fruit of distrust, treachery and intrigue, driven by an evil spirit. Factions and counter-factions rose up, and violence grew in an ever-increasing spiral, ending with the destruction of the city (v45). Finally, Jotham's curse was literally fulfilled when Abimelech set fire to the inner stronghold of Shechem and burnt a thousand people alive (v49), only to meet his own shameful fate at the hands of a woman when he tried to do the same to another city (vv53, 54). This story illustrates principles that are still seen in our time throughout the Middle East. Families and clans stick together, with ties of loyalty that often transcend politics and national goals and lead to widespread nepotism and corruption. And violence always breeds more violence, in an ever-widening cycle of revenge and counter-revenge.

 Pray the Word

Cry out to God in His mercy to break the cycle of violence that builds distrust, hatred and thirst for revenge on both sides of the Israel-Palestinian conflict, and in many Arab nations. Pray for Holy Spirit conviction of the truth that violence hurts its perpetrators more than its victims, and for a release of mercy and forgiveness. *'O LORD…in wrath remember mercy'* (Habakkuk 3:2).

Stand in prayer against the nepotism that prevails in many places and works against economic and political stability, and fuels sectarian violence. *'you have risen up against my father's house this day and have killed his sons...and have made Abimelech …king over the leaders of Shechem, because he is your relative'* (v18).

Pray for an end to idolatry and for the growth of the gospel in all nations of the Middle East, as the only ultimate answer to ongoing violence and sectarianism caused by shedding of blood. Pray especially for Christians to have the grace to forgive. *'Then Jesus said… "Put your sword back into its place. For all who take the sword will perish by the sword"'* (Matthew 26:52).

'And listen to the pleas of your servant and of your people Israel, when they pray toward this place. And listen from heaven your dwelling place, and when you hear, forgive' (2 Chronicles 6:21).

**Passage for study and prayer:
2 Chronicles 6:12-42**

Can we really build God a house? Of course not, said King Solomon, when he prayed and dedicated the great Temple in Jerusalem – He fills the whole universe and beyond, so how could a mere human building, no matter how huge or grand, contain Him (v18)? No, but He had promised to put His name on this house, setting it apart as the focus of worship and relationship with Him (v20). Now Solomon is praying on the basis of God's Word (v17) for the future ministry of the Temple down through the ages. He knows that the LORD is a faithful, covenant-keeping God who will be merciful to those who whole-heartedly love Him (v14). So he prays that this place would always be the epicentre for the prayers of God's people, especially when they needed to repent for their sins, and he beseeches the LORD to hear, forgive and act in response. Whatever the problem – sin against neighbours, defeat by enemies, drought, famine, pestilence or plague – may repentance and prayer bring restored relationship and blessing (vv22-28).

Whether it is a single person or the entire nation, present at the Temple or even looking to it from afar, all have the same access if they come with a repentant heart (vv29, 30). Even foreigners can approach God here in repentance and faith and find out who He truly is (vv32, 33).

Is it surprising then that to a Jew, a part of this ancient Temple site is still the holiest place on earth? Or, that a different religion tries to claim this site as exclusively its own? Today, a small section of the retaining wall of the Second Temple platform is all that survived the Roman destruction in 70 AD – but it is still the place where Jews feel they are closest to God and where He has committed to answer their prayers. Throughout the long centuries of the Diaspora, after Christian and Muslim conquerors had built their temples on the Mount above, Jews came to this Western Wall to weep and pray and plead with God to forgive and restore His people.

Their access was often restricted, but never forbidden, until the Arabs captured and destroyed the Jewish Quarter of the Old City in 1949. Then, all Jews were banned from any kind of access, for 19 years. June 6 1967, when Israeli troops regained the Western Wall and restored the link with 3000 years of spiritual history, was a deeply emotional day for the entire Jewish world. This is why Israel considers East Jerusalem non-negotiable. There is pressure to return to pre-1967 borders in any future peace settlement, but that would mean the unthinkable – handing back the Western Wall.

 Pray the Word

Praise the LORD that the Western Wall is once more the epicentre of Jewish worship and prayer, and ask Him to reveal Himself powerfully to all who sincerely seek Him there. *'Now, O my God, let your eyes be open and your ears attentive to the prayer of this place'* (v40).

Muslim efforts to deny historic Jewish claims to the Temple site have intensified dramatically in the face of ever-increasing archaeological evidence.

Pray that these lies, which actually deny the true God and the Bible, will be exposed, and that the world will fully recognize Israel's unique connection with Jerusalem, *'the place where you have promised to set your name'* (v20).

Pray for God's prophetic purposes for this place to be fulfilled as He overrules in all human decisions, conflicts and circumstances to perform His Will, for His glory. *'You spoke with your mouth, and with your hand have fulfilled it this day'* (v15).

39

'Consider what you do, for you judge not for man but for the LORD. He is with you in giving judgment. Now then, let the fear of the LORD be upon you. Be careful what you do, for there is no injustice with the LORD our God, or partiality or taking bribes' (2Chronicles 19:6, 7)

Passage for study and prayer:
2 Chronicles 19:1-11

Justice is part of God's nature, and very close to his heart. Injustice makes him angry – King Jehoshaphat of Judah was sharply rebuked through God's prophet for supporting a corrupt king of Israel, and afterwards set his heart to please the Lord. His first priority was to act against idolatry and re-establish relationship with God as the basis of justice in his kingdom (vv2-4). Then he appointed judges in each of the chief regional cities to deal with all local civil and criminal matters as God's representatives (v5). They were to exercise judgment with great care and dependence on Him, without partiality, self-seeking or corruption (vv6, 7).

A higher court in Jerusalem, consisting of priests, educated men and prominent elders, would act as an appeal court where necessary and also be responsible for interpreting and deciding legislation (vv8, 10) on the basis of God's word. They would liaise with religious and political leaders, be helped by clerical staff, and aim to keep the nation pleasing God by doing things His righteous way (v11).

Israel's modern democratic judiciary is based on this Biblical model, with regional magistrate courts and a Supreme Court in Jerusalem with judges appointed by the President. However, while it is designed to protect the rights of all citizens, the reality is sometimes less than the ideal. As in other Western states, a strong humanistic influence can sometimes turn justice on its head so that the victim becomes the criminal. On the other hand, Israel is also a Middle Eastern country where influence and 'who knows who' is important and can lead to corruption. The extremely complex security situation complicates issues of justice even further. Israelis themselves complain of political interference in the judiciary, of bias both towards and against religious Jews, of blatant prejudice against Israeli Arabs and other minorities, of favouring Palestinians against Jewish settlers, and the other way around – depending on who you are! There's no doubt some of the accusations are well-founded. Though Israel's justice system is much better than some others in the region, it still falls short of God's high standards.

 Pray the Word

Pray for all justice officials to be completely impartial and above corruption by those who seek to pervert justice for political or religious motives, or for personal gain. *'Now then, let the fear of the LORD be upon you. Be careful what you do, for there is no injustice with the LORD our God, or partiality or taking bribes'* (v7). Pray that prominent political or religious figures who do wrong will not be above the law, either nationally or locally, but will be brought to justice.

Pray for the destruction of all idolatry and humanistic influence within Israel's justice system, especially in the Supreme Court, and a return to Biblical values. Pray for wisdom for judges in all decisions. May they realise the connection between righteousness and God's blessing on the nation, and judge accordingly. *'Thus you shall do in the fear of the LORD, in faithfulness, and with your whole heart: whenever a case comes to you …you shall warn them, that they may not incur guilt before the LORD and wrath may not come upon you and your brothers'* (vv9, 10).

Pray for justice for minorities such as Israeli Arabs, guest workers, refugees, and Messianic believers, who often face discrimination from various quarters. Especially remember believers seeking justice in the courts. *'Deal courageously, and may the LORD be with the upright!'* (v11).

SYRIA AND THE GOLAN

'O mountain of God, mountain of Bashan; O many-peaked mountain, mountain of Bashan! Why do you look with hatred, O many-peaked mountain, at the mount that God desired for his abode, yes, where the LORD will dwell forever?'
(Psalm 68:15, 16)

 Passage for study and prayer: Psalm 68

Bashan is a high plateau to the northeast of Israel, bordering Jordan to the south, stretching north into the Hermon range, and extending eastwards from the Sea of Galilee into Syria. The western portion forms the Golan Heights and upper reaches of the Jordan River. This small piece of territory has always been strategic for Israel, ever since Golan in Bashan was a city of refuge, part of the tribal land of Manasseh. For that reason it has also had a chequered history. In biblical times it swung back and forth between Israel and Syria, often as dictated by dominant regional empires. Jews were resettled there after the Babylonian exile, and archaeological remains testify to the thriving communities that remained until the Arab conquest.

In modern times, Turkish rule gave way to the French Mandate, before the Golan became part of independent Syria in 1946. Israel captured it during the Six Day War in 1967, retained it after the 1974 Yom Kippur War, and brought it under Israeli law in 1981. Syria demands its return under any future peace agreement, whilst most Israelis agree that it is essential for security reasons to keep it, unless real peace is guaranteed.

What makes the Heights so strategic? The simple answer is: war and water. The Golan is an important catchment area and helps feed the Jordan River and the Sea of Galilee, as well as its own fertile soils. Disputes over water were a prelude to war in 1967, when Syria attempted to divert the Jordan's headwaters. After 1949, communities in eastern Galilee also endured frequent shelling from the many Syrian military posts and bunkers on the Heights, along

42

with Palestinian terror raids from Syrian territory. Since Israel pushed the border further north and east, it is no longer overlooked by Syria, but now has its own surveillance stations on Mount Hermon to give early warning of aggression from the north. Israel also now controls the strategic passes onto the Golan. This is vital because Syria actively supports Hizbollah, and is formally allied with Iran against Israel – but disputed land is not the real issue. As this verse from Psalm 68 illustrates, the hatred is based on opposition to God's purposes for Jerusalem, and the inheritance of His people Israel. Praise God, we are assured here of His protection and blessing as He causes His people to inherit the land, and of His revelation and redemption for their enemies too.

 Pray the Word

Give thanks that with the Lord's help, the Golan is no longer a threat but part of Israel's strategic defences. Pray earnestly that it may remain in Israeli hands, for as long as He ordains. *'God shall arise, his enemies shall be scattered; and those who hate him shall flee before him!'* (v1).

Praise God for protecting Israel's water supply, especially important since it now shares water resources with Jordan and the Palestinian territories. *'Rain in abundance, O God, you shed abroad; you restored your inheritance as it languished; your flock found a dwelling in it'* (vv9, 10). Pray for continuing peace and prosperity for Israeli and Druze communities on the Heights, and that Druze in touch with family members in Syria may help change attitudes to Israel there.

Pray for Syria, suffering many political, economic and social problems under the iron rule of the Assad family. Pray for God's Spirit to move powerfully both inside and outside the church, so that Syria, like Cush, *'shall hasten to stretch out her hands to God'* (v31). Pray that the recent film released in Syria about St Paul, produced by Arab Christians and titled *Damascus*, will be used to bring many Arabs to the Lord. *'O kingdoms of the earth, sing to God; sing praises to the Lord'* (v32).

'I have become a stranger to my brothers, an alien to my mother's sons. For zeal for your house has consumed me, and the reproaches of those who reproach you have fallen on me' (Psalm 69:8, 9).

 Passage for study and prayer: Psalm 69:1-33

It can be very dangerous to be a believer in Jesus in the Middle East. In March 2008, on the eve of the festival of Purim, an anonymous gift basket was left on an Israeli Messianic pastor's doorstep. The bomb hidden inside the package critically injured his teenage son. Miraculously, the boy survived, though with horrific injuries needing long term surgical repair and rehabilitation. In late 2009 a religious Jew was arrested who admitted to this crime, motivated by hatred of Jesus and believing he was doing God's will. The resulting publicity emboldened other fanatics, and intimidating death threats against other Jews who believe that Jesus is their Messiah have since increased. Although they had previously suffered harassment, loss of jobs or homes, rejection by family and violent abuse, this attempted murder marked a serious escalation in persecution of the Messianic community. Ultra-Orthodox 'anti-missionaries' are often the well-organized force behind violent demonstrations and propaganda against Israeli believers and their local congregations. They actively seek to change the law in Israel to penalise believers for sharing their faith. There is legal freedom of religion in Israel though it is forbidden to proselytise children or use bribes to win converts.

In the Arab world, persecution of Christians is even more common and severe, especially of those from a Muslim background. Many have died at the hands of family members, or Islamist vigilantes such as those who killed the manager of a Christian bookshop in Gaza in 2007. In most Muslim countries, apostasy from Islam is punishable by death, either through the judicial system or by the local community with tacit consent from the authorities. In Egypt, it is not unusual for members of the sizeable Christian minority to be attacked by Muslim mobs on the slightest pretext. People are killed or injured, homes and businesses are looted and burned. Women are raped, or abducted and forced to marry Muslims and bear Muslim children.

Wooden crosses and Bibles are often burned too, as a direct insult to Jesus and the Christians who bear His name. As Psalm 69 declares, the reproaches which fell upon Jesus now fall on those who love Him. This prayer of David is quoted numerous times in the New Testament as referring prophetically to Jesus and his followers (see for example John 2:17, Luke 23:36, Romans 15:3). It expresses the feelings of those who share in the sufferings of the Messiah and is a great passage of Scripture to pray from as we cry out to God on their behalf.

 Pray the Word

Ask God to help you pray through the verses of this psalm on behalf of those who suffer for their faith throughout the Middle East. Identify with their prayers for help, strength and deliverance, and pray for God's grace to sustain them and for their witness in suffering.

Stand in prayer against false accusations that give the excuse to persecute believers in Jesus. Ask that lies be exposed and that the Lord will work in the hearts of those who are manipulated by them to commit violence. *'More in number than the hairs of my head are those who hate me without cause; mighty are those who would destroy me, those who attack me with lies'* (v4).

Pray that freedom to choose one's faith will be preserved in Israel and all attempts to amend the 'missionary law' will fail. Pray also for a change to the Islamic apostasy law, to give Muslims everywhere freedom to follow Jesus without fear of reprisal. *'Let not those who hope in you be put to shame'* (v6).

THE ENEMIES OF GOD

'For behold, your enemies make an uproar; those who hate you have raised their heads. They lay crafty plans against your people; they consult together against your treasured ones' (Psalm 83:2, 3).

 Passage for study and prayer: Psalm 83

Isn't it amazing how contemporary the Bible is? This psalm is attributed to Asaph, who was the leader of King David's worship team, about a millennium before Jesus was born (1 Chronicles 16). The words are thousands of years old, and yet they could be a response to today's news report. Sadly, the same situation applies today as it did then; Israel is surrounded by enemies who are united in their aim to wipe her out as a nation (vv4, 5). Their tactics are still the same too. They indulge in hate-filled rhetoric via the media, seeking to discredit Israel in every possible way (v2). They lay crafty plans to trap the nation or draw it into retaliation that will be condemned by the world (v3).

The tribes mentioned in verses 6 and 7 are very specific – they all lived on the immediate borders of Israel to the south, east and north and on the coastal plains to the north and southwest. The large and more powerful nation of Assyria was part of the conspiracy too because of its alliance with Moab and Ammon (v8).

Why do they do all this, as much today as over the centuries since David's time? The answer lies in the possessive pronoun! Notice in verse 2, whose enemies they really are. Those who hate God will hate His people, whether they are his ancient covenant people back in His land (note v12), or those around the world who have been brought into the covenant through faith in His son Jesus. This hate has a demonic, spiritual origin. It is interesting that the resurgence of Islamic fundamentalism over the past century or so has coincided with the restoration of Israel as a nation in fulfilment of God's prophetic word, and also with the growth of the church in the non-Western world. Radical Islam fuels the conflict, allowing no place for Israel in the Middle East, and also persecuting Christians, but God has His own plan to turn hate into blessing. Notice the prayer of Asaph in the final verses of this Psalm. Whilst he implores God to act to protect Israel again as He did in the past, he also prays for God's enemies that they may seek and know the LORD as the true God over all the earth, through His dealings with them.

 Pray the Word

Pray through this psalm with specific reference to current events in Israel. Cry out for the LORD to act on behalf of His people, who are his treasured ones, and bring down the spiritual forces of hatred that motivate those who threaten her existence. *'O God, do not keep silence; do not hold your peace or be still, O God!'* (v1). Remind Him of the many times He has saved and delivered Israel and beseech Him to do the same today.

Pray that He will use the forces of nature to protect Israel from attack and to destroy the weapons that have been prepared against her. *'As fire consumes the forest, as the flame sets the mountains ablaze, so may you pursue them with your tempest and terrify them with your hurricane!'* (vv14, 15). Especially think of Iran in this context, with its nuclear capacity alongside the repeated threats of its president to wipe Israel off the face of the earth (v4).

Pray for God's enemies to experience the reality of His power, so that they may seek His face and come to know Him as the true God. *'Fill their faces with shame, that they may seek your name, O LORD... that they may know that you alone, whose name is the LORD, are the Most High over all the earth.'* (vv16, 18) Pray this too in the context of persecuted Christians in the region.

'For he will deliver you from the snare of the fowler and from the deadly pestilence. He will cover you with his pinions, and under his wings you will find refuge; his faithfulness is a shield and buckler' (Psalm 91:3, 4).

 Passage for study and prayer: Psalm 91

Israel's Defence Force has commanders for all its potential battlefronts – the Northern, Central and Southern Commands and, since the Gulf War in 1992, a separate Home Front Command. As a tiny nation in the midst of implacably hostile neighbours, every part of Israel is within reach of enemy missiles and every person becomes a target. The Home Front Command ensures that every citizen knows what to do in case of emergency; be it rocket or missile attack, terrorist bombing or shooting, or natural disasters such as earthquake, flood or fire. Detailed instructions are given in Arabic, Russian and English as well as Hebrew, as to how to prepare for and act in every possible scenario. All Israeli homes contain a designated 'safe room' (in modern houses this is steel-reinforced), in which they keep supplies of food, water, medicines and an emergency bag packed with other necessities. All shared and public buildings have a bomb shelter, and every family trains their children to go instantly to the safest place if the siren sounds, the earth quakes or a bomb explodes nearby.

Israel is probably better prepared for an emergency than any other nation, and indeed shares its expertise frequently at international seminars, and by sending highly trained search and rescue teams to help in disaster situations. However, this psalm reminds us that the Lord Himself is Israel's real refuge. His shelter is better than any bomb shelter, His faithfulness more effective than a missile defence shield. Over and over again, Israelis speak of escapes from danger that are quite miraculous even to those who do not believe or pray.

Those who do, including multitudes of Christians world-wide who intercede for Israel at the Holy Spirit's prompting, know that the Lord's protecting hand is Israel's only real hope against her enemies. He will not let His people be destroyed, for He loves them and they are testimony to His truth and essential to His saving purposes. Today, with hostile nations possessing unconventional, even nuclear, weapons, the threat to Israel's existence has never been more acute. Scientists also warn that a major earthquake is on its way. The Lord wants to use every danger as an opportunity to reveal Himself to as many as have eyes to see, and to further His Kingdom purposes. His angels are waiting to move in response to our prayers!

 Pray the Word

Pray through this psalm for Israel's Home Front. Pray for strength and wisdom for decision-makers, for effective preparedness and equipment, for good coordination of various emergency services – above all, for real trust in God. *'Because you have made the LORD your dwelling place…no evil shall be allowed to befall you, no plague come near your tent. For he will command his angels concerning you, to guard you in all your ways'* (vv9-11).

Claim God's promise for those in the grip of fear, especially in communities close to borders who have been terrorized by persistent rocket attacks in the past. Children in particular have suffered emotional damage. *'You will not fear the terror of the night, nor the arrow that flies by day, nor the pestilence that stalks in darkness, nor the destruction that wastes at noonday'* (vv5, 6). Pray for all Israelis to turn to the LORD in prayer and faith, so that He can reveal His power to them when disaster strikes. *'When he calls to me, I will answer him'* (v15).

Pray particularly for the witness and protection of all believers in Jesus – Jewish, Arab and international, both in Israel and the Palestinian areas – at times of crisis. *'Because he holds fast to me in love, I will deliver him; I will protect him, because he knows my name'* (v14).

49

'I have counsel and sound wisdom; I have insight; I have strength. By me kings reign, and rulers decree what is just' (Proverbs 8:14, 15).

 Passage for study and prayer: Proverbs 8:1-36

It often seems that the whole world stands against Israel, and nothing they do can ever be right. Their leaders frequently find themselves in a Catch-22 situation – damned if they take a particular action, and also damned if they don't. If ever they needed wisdom, the time is now! The Hebrew word for wisdom, *chokhmah,* is from a root meaning 'skill' or 'care', and can be defined as 'skill for living'. It is something that is learned, but it has a divine origin, because it is part of the very character of God. In this chapter, Wisdom is personified as a woman, who has been with God from the beginning and was instrumental in the very creation of the Universe (vv22-31). She is calling out to all who will listen, to learn from her, as she teaches important principles that will lead to life and blessing and the ability to rule wisely and well, so that the people of God may prosper in God's will.

Notice the emphasis on words and speech in many of these verses. The Lord hates evil and perverted speech (v13). Wise words are straight, not twisted, noble not wicked, expressing truth and righteousness (vv6-8). A wise man should learn from the instruction of the whole Word of God, and his speech should reflect this. Yet his actions must be wise too. Prudence and discretion, based on knowledge, are an important part of wisdom (vv5, 12), as are humility, insight and strength of character (vv13, 14) leading to good government (vv15, 16). Wisdom will teach a man to love good, hate evil, and know the difference between the two (vv13, 17, 21). It is far more important and worth pursuing than any earthly treasure (vv 10, 11, 19), but will always bring blessing, material as well as spiritual (v18, 21). Wisdom should not be neglected, but sought diligently, on a daily basis (vv17, 33, 34).

50

Above all, it is rooted in the fear of, implying respect of, and submission to, the LORD (v13).

Jesus, Paul and James in the New Testament distinguish this godly wisdom from earthly wisdom. As they guide the nation into the future, Israel's leaders desperately need to be delivered from the wisdom of this world and be directed by the wisdom from above.

 Pray the Word

Pray the verses of this passage, as the Lord leads you, over Israel's President, Prime Minister and all members of her government. Pray they will seek and find wisdom in the difficult situations they face, and be given grace from God to both speak and act with prudence and integrity, to accomplish His Kingdom purposes. *'And now, O sons, listen to me: blessed are those who keep my ways. Hear instruction and be wise, and do not neglect it'* (vv32, 33).

Pray for wise words for those who speak for Israel in the world's forums; for her diplomats, foreign office officials and media spokesmen. *'Hear, for I will speak noble things, and from my lips will come what is right, for my mouth will utter truth; wickedness is an abomination to my lips'* (vv6, 7). Pray the same for those negotiating with the Palestinians, Syria and other Arab nations.

Pray for the fear of the Lord to fall on all Israel's leaders, including military, religious and local community leadership, to discern and choose what is good rather than evil. *'The fear of the LORD is hatred of evil. Pride and arrogance and the way of evil and perverted speech I hate'* (v13).

Pray that all will be open to receive wise counsel based on God's Word, and that their decisions and policies may reflect godly wisdom. *'The fear of the LORD is the beginning of wisdom, and the knowledge of the Holy One is insight'* (Proverbs 9:10).

'They shall beat their swords into plowshares, and their spears into pruning hooks; nation shall not lift up sword against nation, neither shall they learn war anymore' (Isaiah 2:4).

 Passage for study and prayer: Isaiah 2:1-22

These words are written on the Isaiah Wall in the park just opposite the United Nations Headquarters building in New York, and also alluded to in the 'Let us beat swords into ploughshares' statue presented to the UN by the Soviet Union in 1959. They have come to represent disarmament and many social and political groups promoting global peace – but of course these will never succeed. The quote from verse 4 is incomplete, and all these humanistic organizations ignore the essential ingredient! It is only when the Lord judges between the nations and decides disputes for many peoples, that they are able to turn weapons of war into instruments of peace. The peoples of the earth must first desire to go up to the mountain of the house of the Lord in Jerusalem and learn his ways and walk in his paths, as His Word goes out from Zion (vv2, 3). The restoration of Israel is a step on the way to the final fulfilment of this prophecy when the Prince of Peace returns to rule the earth.

How ironic then that the United Nations, formed to promote peace and harmony between nations and the very instrument God used to found the state of Israel through its vote for partition in 1947, has today become a primary vehicle for the 'new anti-Semitism' which demonises Israel. Those who hate the Jews have gained huge power within the world body, especially in the notorious Human Rights Council that regularly censures Israel whilst ignoring the world's worst abusers. According to UN Watch, an organization which monitors the performance of the UN, the ongoing obsession with Israel is not only so biased it amounts to anti-Semitic propaganda, it deflects huge amounts of time and resources away from other important missions. Such bias also gives tacit support to extremists, so that even though there are more permanent staff and offices dealing with the Palestinian people than any other, no progress is made towards peace, and the radical Hamas and Hizbollah terror groups are able to defy UN resolutions and peacekeepers with impunity in rearming to attack Israel.

Praise God, however, that He will use even the evil schemes of man for his purposes. The rest of this passage is a plea for God's people to repent of their occult practices (v6), their trust in financial and military might (v7) and looking to men for help (v22), and an assurance that the Lord will deal with the pride of men, when He reveals Himself in judgement and glory.

 Pray the Word

Rejoice that the day will come when God's Kingdom rule shall be established and the nations will be truly united in their desire for Him. *'It shall come to pass in the latter days that the mountain of the house of the LORD shall be established as the highest of the mountains, and shall be lifted up above the hills; and all the nations shall flow to it'* (v2).

Pray for the United Nations to be a tool in God's hand, accomplishing His purposes even when it appears to be opposing them. Proclaim to the nations that use and abuse the UN for their own ends that *'the lofty pride of men shall be brought low, and the LORD alone will be exalted in that day'* (v17). Pray for a cleanup of corruption and return to righteous priorities.

Pray that the relentless hatred of the nations will lead Israel back to dependence on God and His Word. *'O house of Jacob, come, let us walk in the light of the LORD'* (v5). May they repent of looking for security in the wrong places, and especially for seeking man's approval. *'Stop regarding man in whose nostrils is breath, for of what account is he?'* (v22).

'And the LORD will strike Egypt, striking and healing, and they will return to the LORD, and he will listen to their pleas for mercy and heal them' (Isaiah 19: 22).

 Passage for study and prayer: Isaiah 19:1-25

Of all Israel's neighbours, Egypt is the most prominent in Scripture, both positively and negatively. She has been a friend and an enemy, a refuge for God's people and a place of slavery and persecution. This wonderful chapter shows how the LORD's fierce judgment on her idols will eventually bring His blessing on her people, who will become part of His heritage and a blessing to the world. Verses 2-16 speak of inter-communal conflict, of spiritual emptiness and economic decline, and of despotic and incompetent leadership, all sent by God in judgment to weaken the nation. They will be in terror of Him and His people Israel, yet in the midst of this turmoil, a scattered remnant will still know and worship the true God (vv17-19). They will cry out to Him to deliver them from their oppressors and He will send a saviour (Hebrew *yasha*) and defender (*rab*), who will also reveal Himself to their fellow countrymen (v20). Unlike their predecessors in the time of Moses, these will respond with sincere worship and repentance. As Egypt is first struck, then healed, its people will know peace with their former enemies Assyria and Israel, and together with them, will become a joint testimony to His grace and salvation.

Notice Israel's key role in this process (v17). In spite of a 'cold peace' that has halted active hostilities for now, it is still hated and feared in Egypt and its very presence on land formerly conquered by Islam, challenges the truth of Islamic theology. Also note that verse 22 says that the Egyptians will **return** to the LORD. For many centuries after St Mark took the gospel to Egypt in the 1st century AD, it was a Christian majority nation, and very influential in the early Christian world. Even after the Arab conquest of 641, the Copts (original Egyptians) were slow to convert to Islam, and a remnant always kept their allegiance to Jesus even under severe persecution. Today, Coptic Orthodox, Catholic or Protestant Christians make up about 10% of the population, and form the largest Christian minority in the Muslim world. In recent decades true spiritual renewal has come to many Christians of all streams, alongside increasing violence and discrimination, often with the collusion of the authorities. There are also growing numbers of Muslims turning to Jesus, although they risk severe persecution. Egypt is the intellectual and theological capital of Islam and this, together with its large Christian community, makes it a major spiritual fault line in the Middle East. This prophesied large-scale spiritual revival will surely shake the whole Islamic world and be a powerful testimony of God's Kingdom!

 Pray the Word

Pray that God will use Egypt's domestic situation, as well as its relationship with Israel, to shake the very foundations of Islamic theology that claims to be the final and only truth. *'In that day the Egyptians will … tremble with fear before the hand that the LORD of hosts shakes over them'* (v16). Pray too for a rediscovery and recognition of Egypt's significant Christian heritage.

Pray for the faithful believers who are standing firm in the midst of persecution. *'When they cry to the LORD because of oppressors, he will send them a saviour and defender, and deliver them. …and the Egyptians will know the LORD in that day'* (vv20, 21). Pray that God will hear their prayers and reveal *Irrab Yasua*, (the Lord Jesus), to them and their Muslim neighbours.

Praise God for Egypt's prophetic destiny in His Kingdom! Pray for the highway of worship and reconciliation to destroy ancient enmities and for the fulfilment of God's promise to make them *'a blessing in the midst of the earth, whom the LORD of hosts has blessed, saying, "Blessed be Egypt my people, and Assyria the work of my hands, and Israel my inheritance"'* (vv24, 25).

'Is it not yet a very little while until Lebanon shall be turned into a fruitful field, and the fruitful field shall be regarded as a forest?' (Isaiah 29:17).

 Passage for study and prayer: Isaiah 29:9-24

Lebanon, the little country north of Israel, was one of the first lands to receive the gospel and until recently, had the largest proportion of Christians in the Middle East. Like Israel, it has known much war and upheaval since independence in 1943. An influx of mostly Muslim Palestinian refugees during the 1948 Arab-Israeli war, and another when members of the Palestinian Liberation Organization were expelled from Jordan in 1971, upset the delicate population and power balance between Christians and Muslims and helped cause the devastating civil war in 1975.

Syria and Israel both became involved and after the war ended in 1990, Israel occupied a southern 'security zone' in an attempt to protect its border from constant terror attack, and the Syrians controlled several proxy governments. The radical Shi'ite Muslim Hizbollah (Army of God), backed by Iran and actively supported by Syria, filled the vacuum left by the removal of PLO forces in 1983 and the final Israeli withdrawal in 2000.

Since the Syrian troops withdrew in 2005, political instability has continued, with several assassinations – and another war between Israel and Hizbollah in 2006 brought fresh destruction and despair. Lebanese Christians, who mostly belong to the ancient Maronite and Eastern Orthodox churches, have left the country in large numbers.

In this passage, we see God's judgment on His people who 'turn things upside down' (v16). Their faith is based on man's understanding, rather than His Word, which they honour with their lips not their hearts (v13). His judgment is to make them spiritually blind and deaf (vv9-12), and to give spiritual truth instead to those who do not have it; as in the picture of the high forested hillsides of Mount Lebanon becoming as fertile and fruitful as the slopes of Carmel ('fruitful field' in Hebrew is *carmel*) and vice versa (v17). The next verses contain the wonderful promise that God's good news will spread beyond his own people, to the needy of all mankind (v19). Those without God's word will read it (v18), those who submit to Him will be filled with fresh joy (v19) and evildoers will be cut off (v20). Best of all, His mercy extended to those outside the covenant will bring fresh life to those within it too, as the Holy One of Jacob is exalted and all who go astray in spirit come to understanding (vv22-24). What excellent verses to pray for war-torn Lebanon, where the Lord wants to bring spiritual fruit in a climate of political turmoil and reach Christians and Muslims alike with fresh, life-giving truth and faith from His Word, by His Spirit!

 Pray the Word

Proclaim the promise of v 17 over Lebanon and pray for the fulfilment of all God's purposes in this strategic nation. Pray that difficult times may open ears and eyes of all sections of society to God's Word of truth and hope. *'In that day the deaf shall hear the words of a book, and out of their gloom and darkness the eyes of the blind shall see'* (v18).

Pray for a fresh outpouring of the Holy Spirit upon the remnant church in Lebanon, that they may be strengthened to reach out to the needy in their midst. *'The meek shall obtain fresh joy in the LORD, and the poor among mankind shall exult in the Holy One of Israel'* (v19).

Stand in prayer against the rising power of Hizbollah, both militarily and politically. *'For the ruthless shall come to nothing and the scoffer cease, and all who watch to do evil shall be cut off, who by a word make a man out to be an offender and lay a snare for him who reproves in the gate'* (vv20, 21). Pray for a securing of the porous border with Syria, and an end to Syrian support for Hizbollah and interference in Lebanese affairs.

'It is too light a thing that you should be my servant to raise up the tribes of Jacob and to bring back the preserved of Israel; I will make you as a light for the nations, that my salvation may reach to the end of the earth' (Isaiah 49:6)

 Passage for study and prayer: Isaiah 49:1-13

In the Bible, Israel is both a person and a people. Jacob the patriarch became Israel after he wrestled with God, and in Egypt, his descendants became a nation. We know that Isaiah's famous Servant Song describes Messiah Jesus, God's chosen Servant, who would bring His salvation not only to the elect of Israel but also to Gentiles of all nations - yet it also speaks of the restored nation of Israel. From the start Israel was chosen to be God's servant, revealing His glory to other nations through His dealings with them. Israel calls the attention of the world to the LORD (v1). For many years the Jewish people were dispersed and out of sight, hidden in God's hand - yet He was preparing them for His purposes, as they trusted in His promises (vv2-4). Those purposes were two-fold; to raise up and restore the remnant of Israel, and to shine light and salvation to the nations (vv5-6).

That the restoration is to the land as well as to the Lord is made very clear from verses 8-12, which could easily be a description of Israel's recent history. As its people have returned from north, south, east and west under God's hand to establish the land and prosper there, they have indeed been a beacon of light to others.

How can this be? Hasn't Israel's restoration actually brought suffering and war? Yes it has, to those who have resisted it, and to Israelis too, but in far more ways it has been a blessing. Having to survive against the odds and overcome many difficulties has led to discoveries and inventions that have benefited their region and far beyond it. From drip irrigation and solar power to electronic communications and medical research, Israel has led the way for the rest of us. As global warming and carbon emissions threaten the health of our planet, Israel is now pioneering new energy sources and green technology.

The goal and ethos of being a light to the nations has also made tiny Israel reach out to help others, whether through development programmes in Africa, cardiac surgery for Arab children, or aid in natural disasters. Above all, God's promise of spiritual restoration to Israel is being fulfilled, and the blessing is spilling out worldwide. Since 1948, more Jews in Israel and elsewhere have come to faith in Jesus the Messiah than in the previous 1900 years. In the same period there has been unprecedented church growth in Latin America, Asia, Africa, and especially in the hard fields of the Muslim world. This is all God's plan and His doing, though most Israelis still believe they have achieved it on their own!

 Pray the Word

Pray that Israelis will not lift themselves up in pride at what they have achieved in fulfilling the Jewish ideal of *tikkun olam,* 'repairing the world', but may remember that it is because of the Lord's favour, and for His glory: *'You are my servant, Israel, in whom I will be glorified'* (v3).

Praise God for all that He has done to bless the world through modern Israel in its short history. Pray that the nations will recognize and appreciate its contribution, and be drawn to seek its God: *'Kings shall see and arise; princes, and they shall prostrate themselves; because of the LORD, who is faithful, the Holy One of Israel, who has chosen you'* (v7).

Pray that Jews still remaining in other nations will be brought home to fulfil their destiny. Pray especially for those who still remain to the north of Israel, in the Islamic states of Turkey, Syria, Iran and the central Asian former Soviet republics, and for those in western nations. *'I will make all my mountains a road, and my highways shall be raised up. Behold, these shall come...from the north and from the west'* (vv11-12).

'For as the rain and the snow come down from heaven and do not return there but water the earth, making it bring forth and sprout, giving seed to the sower and bread to the eater, so shall my word be that goes out from my mouth; it shall not return to me empty, but it shall accomplish that which I purpose, and shall succeed in the thing for which I sent it' (Isaiah 55:10, 11).

 Passage for study and prayer: Isaiah 55:1-13

In Israel, it is impossible not to be conscious of the Bible – the entire country is a testament to both the Old and the New Covenant Scriptures. Often called 'the fifth Gospel', the land illuminates its context, illustrates its geography and verifies its history through hundreds of archaeological digs and sites going back at least three thousand years. Christians who visit find the Bible comes alive in a new way and many have found a fresh relationship with the Scriptures and the Lord while walking in the footsteps of Jesus and the prophets.

One of the wonderful by-products for the Jewish people of their return to their ancestral homeland, has been a renewed interest in the Scriptures themselves, as opposed to merely studying the commentaries and wisdom of the rabbis. This interest includes the New Testament, which is increasingly recognized as an authentic first-century collection of Jewish texts, and is studied in many universities and seminaries both as history and as literature.

Today, anyone in Israel has easy access to a complete Bible in Hebrew, Arabic or indeed many other languages. The Bible Society in Israel has bookshops in Jerusalem and Tel Aviv as well as an associated Arab Israeli Society in Nazareth, and the Palestinian Bible Society has branches in eight centres in the West Bank and Gaza. All these, together with a number of church-based bookshops in other major cities, are involved in providing not only the Scriptures and other literature but reaching out in various ways to their communities. All testify of the hunger for the Word of God amongst many needy people, especially in the south of Israel, and in the Palestinian areas, where the ongoing conflict has had the most impact. They report frequent conversations about the New Testament with curious people from all walks of life, even the notoriously hostile ultra-orthodox community.

 Pray the Word

Give thanks that the Bible is freely available in Israel and the Palestinian territories and pray that the Lord will speak wherever and whenever it is read. Proclaim in prayer the wonderful truth that God's Word will always accomplish what He purposes (vv10, 11).

Pray for the many Bible bookshops in various centres, and for their staff, with all the opportunities they have for witness and outreach. *'Come, everyone who thirsts, come to the waters; and he who has no money, come, buy and eat!'* (v1). Pray for protection from radical religious elements, especially for those in the West Bank and Gaza, and for a great harvest of repentance and faith. *'Let the wicked forsake his way, and the unrighteous man his thoughts; let him return to the LORD, that he may have compassion on him, and to our God, for he will abundantly pardon'* (v7).

Pray for orthodox Jews studying in *yeshivot* (seminaries) to be enlightened by the Holy Spirit to hear and respond to the truth of God's word where it has been obscured by rabbinic teaching. *'Incline your ear, and come to me; hear, that your soul may live; and I will make with you an everlasting covenant...For my thoughts are not your thoughts, neither are your ways my ways, declares the LORD'* (vv3, 8).

Pray too that professors and students academically studying the New Testament will have a powerful, personal encounter with Jesus.

GOD'S ROYAL CROWN

'You shall also be a crown of beauty in the hand of the LORD, and a royal diadem in the hand of your God.' (Isaiah 62:3)

 Passage for study and prayer: Isaiah 62:1-12

Would you imagine, as you see yet another news report from conflict-ridden Jerusalem, that this city is destined to be God's royal crown - the adornment and symbol of His kingly majesty? Yet the truth is that Jerusalem's unique destiny is actually the root of all the problems, as every anti-God spiritual force that opposes His Kingdom focuses on trying to steal and destroy this precious jewel in every possible way. How wonderful that the LORD is not about to allow this! In the Hebrew, verse 3 uses two words for 'hand' – '*yad*' the open upheld hand of authority, and then '*kaf*', the protective palm of the hand. It is God's power and ceaseless protection, never remaining silent or inactive, that will see Jerusalem finally fulfil her prophetic destiny as a city of righteousness and salvation (v1), redeemed by the LORD and sought out by the Gentiles because of her bright reflection of His glory (vv2, 12).

Yet the LORD chooses not to accomplish this alone. He has called watchmen to help protect and prepare His crown by constantly reminding Him to fulfil His promise to make Jerusalem a praise in all the earth (vv6, 7). The Hebrew word used here for 'watchmen' is shomrim, but in Jeremiah31:6 it is notzrim, and interestingly, *notzrim* is the modern Hebrew word for 'Christians'! Just as Jerusalem has a calling to reflect God's glory to the nations, so believers in Israel's God round the world have a calling to watch vigilantly over her in prayer and proclaim to her that her destiny will be fulfilled, through God's power, no matter how unlikely or impossible it may seem.

Through the prayers of past generations of Christians, verses 4 and 5 have already been partly fulfilled. In 1839 Jerusalem was poor and desolate, as Scottish pastors Andrew Bonar and Robert Murray McCheyne testified when they visited, but today's tourists find a vibrant, beautiful city that has blossomed since Jews have returned in numbers to renew their covenant relationship with the Holy City. Jerusalem is now the capital of Israel, in control of its own economy (vv8, 9) and also experiencing a measure of spiritual restoration. However peace, righteousness and full salvation have not yet arrived. As watchmen, we must proclaim to Jerusalem that her salvation, *yesha*, is coming (v11). Did you know that Jesus' name in Hebrew is *Yeshua*, meaning 'salvation of Yahweh'? The return of the Messiah to the city where His life was given for the salvation of mankind will be the final fulfilment of Jerusalem's prophetic destiny.

 Pray the Word

Praise and proclaim in prayer and faith that God will accomplish every one of His promises to Jerusalem given in these verses, because *'The LORD has sworn by His right hand and by the arm of His strength'* (v8). The Hebrew here is extremely emphatic!

Plead with the Lord to call many more watchmen worldwide to pray for Jerusalem as the conflict over God's special city intensifies in the coming days. *'On your walls, O Jerusalem, I have set watchmen; all the day and all the night they shall never be silent'* (v12). Pray for Holy Spirit anointing to engage in the spiritual battle. *'Take...the sword of the Spirit, which is the Word of God, praying at all times in the Spirit'* (Ephesians 6:17, 18).

Pray for the removal of all obstacles to full salvation, including false religious spirits, for the citizens of Jerusalem, both Jewish and Arab. Pray for the revelation of Yeshua as Messiah of all. *'And they shall call them The Holy People, the Redeemed of the LORD'* (v12).

'And it shall come to pass, if they will diligently learn the ways of my people, to swear by my name, "As the LORD lives," even as they taught my people to swear by Baal, then they shall be built up in the midst of my people' (Jeremiah 12:16).

 Passage for study and prayer: Jeremiah 12:14-17

When the Lord restored Israel a second time to her inheritance in the last century, those already living there had a choice – either to embrace the Jews who were returning, and benefit from the new opportunities their coming brought, or to fear and even violently reject them. Not all Arabs living in the new state of Israel in 1948 became part of the mass exodus of Palestinian refugees; about 20% stayed and took their chance on the Israeli promise of full rights as a minority in a Jewish state. Numbering approximately 150,000 in 1948, their numbers swelled in 1967 with the addition of residents of East Jerusalem and four Druze villages on the Golan. Today, 1.5 million Israeli Arabs comprise 20.3% of Israel's population. They consist of Christians, Druze and Muslims, including the nomadic Bedouin of the Negev desert. Some live in their own towns and villages, others alongside Jews in mixed communities, especially in the larger cities. They share fully in the benefits of Israel's democracy, with the vote and equal access to welfare services, although there has been long-term discrimination and the Arab sector is generally poorer and has fewer public funds allocated to education and civic amenities, leading to many social problems.

The Israeli Arab community has indeed been built up in the midst of His people, but the most important part of this prophecy is yet to be fully accomplished, as the Lord desires to bless them most through knowing Him. Israel is the only nation in the Middle East where the Christian population has increased over the past 60 years. There is freedom of religion and today, many Muslims are braving the opposition of family and community to turn to Jesus – there are even a few believers amongst the Druze, a closed Muslim sect which formerly has been very resistant to the gospel. Some fellowships have Jewish and Arab believers serving God together as a living testimony to reconciliation through Jesus. Sadly, generally good relationships have been soured in recent years by the Palestinian uprisings, which have led to a serious breakdown in trust, and to Israeli fears about a 'fifth column', and the 'demographic time bomb' of the higher Arab birthrate which could eventually destroy Israel's Jewish identity. The Islamic Movement is growing and many younger Arab Israelis are identifying more with the Palestinian cause, though most insist they do not want to live under Palestinian rule in any future exchange of territory.

 Pray the Word

Give thanks for Israel's Arab community, which in spite of problems has proved the benefit of a genuine democracy. Pray that they may prosper economically and especially spiritually in the Jewish state, as a testimony to the rest of the Arab world. *'They shall be built up in the midst of my people. But if any nation will not listen, then I will utterly pluck it up and destroy it'* (vv16, 17).

Pray for an end to prejudice and unfair discrimination, especially against young Arabs who may struggle to gain higher education, jobs and housing. *'You shall treat the stranger who sojourns with you as the native among you, and you shall love him as yourself'* (Leviticus 19:34). Pray that they may not fall prey to political and Islamic radicals, but will desire to live in peace. *'Turn away from evil and do good; seek peace and pursue it'* (Psalm 34:14).

Pray for protection for believers from a Muslim or Druze background, and that they may be built up in the faith, finding unity both with Christian Arabs and Messianic Jews, and being a powerful witness in their own communities. *'Behold, how good and pleasant it is when brothers dwell in unity! For there the LORD has commanded the blessing, life forevermore'* (Psalm 133:1, 3).

'I am handing you over to the people of the East for a possession, and they shall set their encampments among you and make their dwellings in your midst' (Ezekiel 25:4).

 Passage for study and prayer: Ezekiel 25:1-11

Amman is the capital of modern Jordan, and it is an ancient city. It was once the capital of the Ammonites, Israel's distant cousins through Abraham's nephew Lot, who were amongst their most implacable enemies. Jordan also encompasses the ancient territories of Moab, Ammon's brother, and of Edom the son of Esau. All these peoples lost their national identity in fulfilment of this prophecy, under judgment from God because of their treatment of His people Israel. Their lands were settled by Arabs, the nomadic 'people of the East', whose caravan routes traversed this area en route to the north, east and west. The most famous of these were the wealthy Nabateans, who controlled the spice routes for centuries and whose magnificent rock city of Petra is one of Jordan's foremost tourist attractions. Under the Ottomans Jordan was part of Palestine, and then became Transjordan under the British Mandate after World War I, in preparation for independence as an Arab state. In 1946, Prince Abdullah of the Hashemites, at that time the ruling family in Arabia, became King of the independent Hashemite Kingdom of Jordan.

This territory given by God to the Arabs has continued to be closely entwined with Israel. More than half Jordan's citizens are descendants of hundreds of thousands of Palestinians who fled Israel in 1948-49, or from the West Bank in 1967, and many are still strongly antagonistic to the Jewish state. The government dealt firmly with radical Palestinian elements in 1970 and avoided further direct wars with Israel, quietly moving towards peace under the pragmatic leadership of King Hussein. A peace treaty was signed in 1994 and since then there has been much unobtrusive cooperation between them, as they share both a border and water resources.

Today, Jordan is still a pro-Western constitutional monarchy under King Abdullah II, which aims to keep the peace with all of its more volatile neighbours. However, new waves of refugees have flooded in from the east following the wars in Kuwait and Iraq, and it is estimated that there are now well over a million Iraqi refugees dwelling amongst the Jordanians, seriously straining the country's resources and threatening to destabilise it politically. About 15% are Christians, adding to the existing Christian minority, which currently enjoys a small measure of religious freedom and provides a strategic base for Christian mission and leadership training in the Arab world.

 Pray the Word

Praise God that Jordan has made peace with Israel, and pray fervently for God's protection on that peace, and on their shared border: *'Turn away from evil and do good; seek peace and pursue it'* (Psalm 34:14). Pray for continuing political stability and growing economic prosperity, especially in the light of the problems arising from the recent influx of refugees.

Pray that as a moderate Muslim state, Jordan will have a positive influence in the Arab world. Pray for wisdom for the King and elected leaders in their regional relationships, and especially with the Palestinian leadership. Pray earnestly for Jordan's protection from extremist Islamist elements that would seek to destabilise the country for their own ends. *'For they do not speak peace, but against those who are quiet in the land they devise words of deceit'* (Psalm 35:20).

Give thanks that Jordan's dwindling Christian minority has been strengthened by Iraqi Christians, and pray for them all *'that the God of our Lord Jesus Christ, the Father of glory, may give you a spirit of wisdom and of revelation in the knowledge of him'* (Ephesians 1:17). Pray for even more freedom to share the gospel, and for the strengthening of the church through effective leadership and ministry training.

"'Because you cherished perpetual enmity [ancient hatred] and gave over the people of Israel to the power of the sword at the time of their calamity... therefore, as I live", declares the Lord GOD, "I will prepare you for blood, and blood shall pursue you"' (Ezekiel 35:5, 6).

 Passage for study and prayer: Ezekiel 35:1-15

Mount Seir is in Edom, the ancient homeland of Esau, Jacob's older brother who sold him his birthright. Throughout Scripture, the Edomites were bitter enemies of Israel. Ezekiel speaks here of how they took advantage of the situation when Nebuchadnezzar invaded Judah, to aid the enemy and then after the exile to Babylon, to settle the land. The Lord is very angry with them, on several counts. Firstly, they cherished perpetual enmity (v5), keeping their ancient hatred alive by nurturing it and passing it on to their children and expressing it by rejoicing in the shedding of Israel's blood (v6). Secondly, they never ceased coveting the lands of both Judah and Israel, failing to acknowledge God's presence and purposes, and driven by anger and envy (vv10, 11). Thirdly, they spoke evil words against the land and against God (vv12, 13). For all these things, the Lord will turn their sin back on themselves, and their blood will be shed, their land made desolate, their inheritance destroyed (vv6-9). In doing this, however, He as always has a redemptive purpose – to reveal to them that He is the true God (vv4, 9, 11, 12, 15).

God's judgment fell and the Edomites are no more, but their attitudes live on today in the Arab world, fuelled by Islamic theology. Jews and Arabs were not always enemies. Jewish communities lived peacefully in 7th century Arabia and initially Muhammad was open towards them, as reflected in the earlier verses of the Quran. However, this changed after Arabian Jews refused to convert to his new religion. Later (and therefore more authoritative) Quranic verses, as well as parts of the Hadith, (sayings and deeds of Muhammad), are virulently anti-Semitic and openly call for the death of Jews. Such teaching is prominent in the education system in the Arab world and fosters a climate of hatred and distrust against Israel from babyhood. School textbooks and children's TV as well as public media and religious broadcasts, all demonise the Jewish people and glorify the concept of 'jihad', or holy war, against them. No wonder peace is elusive – in Islamic theology, unless Islam rules Israel once more, it is impossible!

But there is hope. God will both judge, and He will save, as he did the Edomites (Idumeans in Greek). They lived south of Judea and finally lost their separate identity when they acknowledged the LORD and converted to become part of God's covenant people, a few generations before Jesus was born.

 Pray the Word

Praise God that the stronghold of Islam will yield to His Kingdom in due time! Pray with all your heart for an end to Islamic anti-Semitism, with its cycle of hatred and bloodshed that brings such judgment and suffering to those held captive by it: *'because you did not hate bloodshed, therefore blood shall pursue you'* (v6). Pray for Muslims to be so sickened by perpetual enmity that they will long for peace, love and forgiveness, and find them all in Jesus the Jewish Messiah.

Pray for Palestinians that their sufferings will lead them to the true God and His salvation. For those who have grown up as stateless exiles in refugee camps, or in constant conflict with Israel, the ancient hatred has been fertilised even more by the pain of their own situations. *'I will lay your cities waste, and you shall become a desolation, and you shall know that I am the LORD'* (v4).

Pray especially for the youth of the West Bank and Gaza, brainwashed from infancy to hate the Jews and embrace a lifestyle of violence. Pray for all who seek to help them and for deliverance and healing of this generation through access to the truth. *'So it is not the will of my Father who is in heaven that one of these little ones should perish'* (Matthew 18:14).

GRAVES OF THE HOLOCAUST

'Therefore prophesy, and say to them, "Thus says the Lord GOD: 'Behold, I will open your graves and raise you from your graves, O my people. And I will bring you into the land of Israel'" (Ezekiel 37:12).

 Passage for study and prayer: Ezekiel 37:1-15

Visitors to Israel's haunting and powerful Holocaust Museum, Yad Vashem, can't miss the enormous words chiselled in English and Hebrew on a huge concrete arch over the entrance. They are from this passage: *'I will put My breath into you and you shall live again, and I will set you upon your own soil'* (v14, JPS). Everyone in Israel and also in the Arab world knows that the Nazi Holocaust during World War Two was the catalyst that finally led to the formation of the Jewish state. Israel arose from the graves of the 6 million Jews that perished during Hitler's "Final Solution to the Jewish Problem". The living skeletons finally liberated from the death camps, and the ones and twos that had escaped to hide undetected, formed a pitiful remnant of European Jewry that swung world opinion and the vote at the United Nations to partition the British Mandate of Palestine between its Arab and Jewish residents, so that at last, after thousands of years, the Jews could again be secure in their own land.

It couldn't have happened without God. Resurrection is His prerogative, as Ezekiel realised (v3) – only the LORD was able to bring life to those very dry bones he saw in the valley. As the prophet was obedient to declare God's Word of resurrection promise over them, he saw the bones begin to move, to join together, to be linked with sinews and covered by flesh and skin, until they were bodies again. Yet still those bodies were dead. They needed the wind to come from the four corners of the earth to breathe upon them and only then did they stand up as a living, breathing army. This was the people of Israel (v11). In exile from their covenant land, they were lifeless bones of a nation – yet here was the promise that new life was possible by the breath or spirit of God, in response to His Word. The words translated as breath, wind and spirit in this passage are all the same Hebrew word, *ruach*.

The Holy Spirit is *Ruach HaKodesh*, and it is only by His power that the spiritual restoration of Israel will be completed and its people will fully know the LORD (vv6,13, 14). This is the ultimate goal, and not for Israel's sake only, for as Paul says in Romans 11:15, *'If their rejection means the reconciliation of the world, what will their acceptance mean but life from the dead?'*

 Pray the Word

Praise the LORD for Israel's restoration to the land and proclaim in prayer that its ultimate purpose, the spiritual renewal of His people, will be fully completed: *'And I will put my Spirit within you, and you shall live, and I will place you in your own land. Then you shall know that I am the LORD; I have spoken, and I will do it, declares the LORD'* (v14).

Pray for the remaining survivors of the trauma of the Holocaust, and their descendants, all deeply affected by the emotional scars they suffered. *'Thus says the Lord GOD: Come from the four winds, O breath, and breathe on these slain, that they may live'* (v9). Pray for those who seek to minister God's love and healing to them.

Stand in prayer against all Holocaust denial. Many Arabs deny the facts and true horror of the Holocaust in their anger and bitterness over the ongoing suffering of Palestinian refugees, whom they consider are victims of European guilt. To them, Israel's restoration is the *Nakhba*, or Catastrophe. Above all, pray for a great spiritual revival amongst Palestinians as part of God's wider plan. *'For this is the will of my Father, that everyone who looks on the Son and believes in him should have eternal life, and I will raise him up on the last day'* (John 6:40).

71

'And I will make them one nation in the land, on the mountains of Israel. And one king shall be king over them all, and they shall be no longer two nations, and no longer divided into two kingdoms' (Ezekiel 37:22).

 Passage for study and prayer: Ezekiel 37:16-28

Unity is a powerful force – after all, it is part of the very nature of God. The opposite is true too; the kingdoms of Israel and Judah were both weakened by their division after Solomon's reign. The Lord's purpose is always to unify, as Ezekiel's powerful visual aid, uniting two sticks named 'Israel' and 'Judah' in his fist, demonstrated to the Babylonian exiles (v17). God's divided people will one day be joined in His hand, gathered by Him back to their own land as one nation on the mountains of Israel, encompassing the territory of both Judah and Israel. Their unity will come from their cleansing by God from all idolatry and sin (v23), their submission to God's Word, and to the authority of 'my servant David', the Messiah, who will be their shepherd and King in the land the LORD has given them (v24). Note the intertwined relationship in verses 25-28 between the people, the Land, the Messiah, and the LORD, and notice too that the Hebrew expression *olam olam,* translated variously here as 'forever', 'everlasting', and 'forevermore', occurs five times in total! A new 'for ever and ever' covenant of peace will finally fully restore relationship with God, and will reveal Him to the nations as He dwells in the midst of His people.

This prophecy partly came to pass at the end of the first exile, when the Judeans (or 'Jews') returned and absorbed those Israelites who remained in or had straggled back to the northern kingdom of Israel. Centuries later, *Yeshua,* Son of David, came and inaugurated the promised Messianic Kingdom and the covenant of peace, yet

He Himself taught that it still has a future and final consummation. Surely, the return of the people of Israel in modern times to their homeland is a further step towards the final, forever fulfilment of this promise. As they come home from all over the world, the Jewish people are divided by many things – language, culture, politics, and religious doctrines (or lack of them!)

Whilst the resurrected Hebrew language is a unifying factor for new immigrants, as is education and army service, divisions in Israeli society remain deep and are of great concern. In the past, disunity was a major cause of Jerusalem's fall, first to Nebuchadnezzar of Babylon and then to the Romans five centuries later. To stay strong, Israel needs to be united, but we know that lasting unity will only come with repentance, submission to God's Word and supremely, to His Messiah.

 Pray the Word

Praise God that the supreme purpose for which He has restored the people of Israel to their Land is to come and dwell with them! Pray for the presence of God to be manifest amongst them, as they face the challenges of their daily lives. *'My dwelling place shall be with them, and I will be their God, and they shall be my people'* (v27).

Pray for God to convict of pride, selfish interests, racism, religious sectarianism, and all idolatry leading to disunity, and bring true repentance to all sections of society. *'But I will save them from all the backslidings in which they have sinned, and will cleanse them'* (v23).

Pray especially for deep and sincere unity amongst the believers in Israel. Their different congregations may reflect the diversity of the nation, but their unity is a powerful witness, hence often under attack by the enemy. *'My servant David shall be king over them, and they shall all have one shepherd'* (v24).

73

'After many days you will be mustered. In the latter years you will go against the land that is restored from war, the land whose people were gathered from many peoples upon the mountains of Israel, which had been a continual waste. Its people were brought out from the peoples and now dwell securely, all of them' (Ezekiel 38:8).

 Passage for study and prayer: Ezekiel 38:1-23

This famous prophecy about Gog and Magog and their future war against Israel seems as yet to be unfulfilled. There are many different views about the precise modern identity of Gog and the various nations mentioned here, but some things are very clear. An alliance of various countries will build up against Israel over a long period. A massive invasion from the north, under Gog's leadership, will take place after the land has been restored and is prospering under its people who have returned from around the world. Although these enemies will come against God's people because they judge them to be vulnerable, and because they covet the prosperity they have gained, in fact it is the Lord Himself who will draw them there in order to judge them and in doing so, to reveal His holiness to the entire earth. They will be an enormously powerful army, well-equipped and huge in number, but the Lord will defeat them Himself with a huge earthquake and other natural disasters, as well as disease and confusion in their ranks that will cause many to die at each other's hands in 'friendly fire'.

Some of the nations mentioned are easily identifiable, such as Persia, which only became Iran in 1935. Others are more vague, but would seem from other Bible passages to include Egypt and/or Libya or Somalia (Cush and Put). All of them are Islamic countries which are openly anti-Israel. Interestingly, Gomer and Togarmah refer to modern Turkey, at present the only officially secular and most democratic Muslim state in the Middle East. Turkey recognised Israel back in 1949 and has been its only regional ally.

They share trade agreements and cooperate on defence. Israel sells arms to Turkey, and Israelis flock to Turkish holiday resorts. The relationship in fact goes back centuries, as multitudes of Jews fleeing Spain during the Inquisition found refuge there, and today it has the only sizeable Jewish population still remaining in the region outside Israel.

However, there are signs this is changing. Islamic pressure is mounting from within against the secular constitution. Turkey's unsuccessful attempt to join the EU has caused it to look east rather than west, and Israel's confrontation with Hamas in Gaza in 2009 led to a marked cooling of relations and increase in anti-Semitic propaganda. Suddenly, the Ezekiel 38 scenario seems a lot more possible, with powerful Turkey to the north of Israel perhaps becoming the rallying point for the combined armies of Islam, in what will be the final jihad.

 Pray the Word

Pray for Turkey's government and people at this time of massive change when the forces of Islam are on the rise against the pro-Western secular foundation of the state. Pray for God to overrule all that happens there for His purposes. *'And I will turn you about and put hooks into your jaws, and I will bring you out'* (v4).

Pray for Turkey's Jewish community, about 25,000 strong, to have wisdom and protection from God in the changing situation and be drawn to return to Israel before persecution begins. *"I will whistle for them and gather them in, for I have redeemed them"* (Zechariah 10:8).

Pray for Turkish Christian converts, who still face great opposition and danger in a country that has had a terrible history of severe persecution against Christians in the past. Pray for their witness, and for God's mercy in the midst of judgment, so that millions in Turkey may come to know Him in the times ahead. *'So I will show my greatness and my holiness and make myself known in the eyes of many nations. Then they will know that I am the LORD'* (v23).

THE PRINCE OF PERSIA

'Then he said to me, "Fear not, Daniel, for from the first day that you set your heart to understand and humbled yourself before your God, your words have been heard, and I have come because of your words. The prince of the kingdom of Persia withstood me twenty-one days, but Michael, one of the chief princes, came to help me"' (Daniel 10:12, 13).

 Passage for study and prayer: Daniel 10:1-21

This passage gives us a valuable glimpse into what happens in the spiritual world when we fast and pray. Daniel still lived in exile in Babylonia, now ruled by Cyrus King of Persia, even though some exiles had returned to Jerusalem to rebuild the temple and were meeting with great opposition (see Ezra 1:1, 4:1-5). In his old age Daniel devoted himself to seeking God for knowledge of and fulfilment of His purposes for his people, according to His Word. The Lord had already given him some amazing angelic revelations, but this time he had been fasting and praying for three whole weeks before anything happened. Why? There had been a great spiritual battle going on (v1), and his fasting and prayer were part of it.

The mighty angelic being that finally appeared to him on the banks of the Tigris had been on his way ever since Daniel started praying, but had been delayed by a 'prince of Persia' who had fought him for 21 days, until 'Michael, one of the chief princes' came to help him (v13). Clearly there are good and bad angels or 'princes' in the spiritual realm, who either carry out the business of God's Kingdom or oppose it with all in their power. This angel was God's special messenger of revelation, quite possibly Gabriel, who had visited Daniel twice before. Michael the archangel is the warrior-prince identified with God's people (v21). Likewise the princes of Persia and Greece are demonic powers with influence over specific people groups, and particularly their secular rulers,

76

whose decisions affect the destiny of God's people. (Note verse 13's reference to the kings of Persia).

It seems that Persia's ruling principality wanted both to stop Daniel receiving revelation that he (and future generations) could use as prayer fuel, and also to interfere with the practical answers to his prayers on the ground in Jerusalem. Daniel in Babylon, Cyrus in Persia, Ezra in Jerusalem – they were all involved with the spiritual warfare over God's agenda for Israel and His Kingdom. Daniel seemed far from the action, yet his humble, selfless, and persistent intercession was the key to victory.

 ## Pray the Word

Pray for your church and the church worldwide to receive Holy Spirit revelation of Biblical truth concerning God's end-time purposes for Israel and the nations. *'I… came to make you understand what is to happen to your people in the latter days. For the vision is for days yet to come'* (v14). Pray this especially for believers in Israel and in the Arab world.

Beseech the Lord to call and empower many more intercessors willing to pay the sometimes heavy price to fast and pray in a spirit of humility and dependence on God. *"'O man greatly loved, fear not, peace be with you; be strong and of good courage." And as he spoke to me, I was strengthened and said, "Let my lord speak, for you have strengthened me"'* (v19).

Pray fervently for Iran (formerly Persia) where Shiite Islamist leaders are developing nuclear weapons and aim to destroy the nation of Israel, along with their quest to bring the Islamic Mahdi (Messiah) to rule the entire world. Pray for angelic reinforcements to battle the prince of Persia as he seeks to usurp God's kingdom purposes. *'[the Most High] does according to his will among the host of heaven and among the inhabitants of the earth; and none can stay his hand or say to him, "What have you done?"'* (Daniel 4:35). Pray for a tsunami of prayer to overwhelm Iran in these crucial days, to protect its people, and bring multitudes to faith in Jesus.

'And I said to her, "You shall stay with me many days; you shall not play the harlot, nor shall you have a man – so too will I be toward you"' (Hosea 3:3, NKJV).

 Passage for study and prayer: Hosea 3:1-5

When God called Hosea to be a prophet to Israel, the first thing He told him to do was to marry a prostitute and have children with her (see Hosea 1:2-9). His family life was to be a picture of God's faithful love for His unfaithful wife Israel – though He will judge her for her unfaithfulness (2:2-13), His everlasting love will in the end woo her to repentance (2:14-23). In short chapter 3, Hosea speaks again of his own experience; in stark prose rather than poetry, conveying something of his personal pain. His wife had left him for other lovers, just as Israel had looked to other gods, and now the Lord tells him to find her and love her all over again (v1).

He has to pay a price to redeem her, for she had sold herself into slavery (v2). This time he sets her some new rules. She is to stay with him alone, no more running around with other men – in fact verse 3 could infer that she will not have intimate relations even with himself, for the time being. He will lovingly care for her in every way, but until his faithful love wins her love in return, and they have a real, reciprocal relationship as God intended, they will not know the deepest intimacy and blessing of marriage. That is still in the future.

Verses 4 and 5 then speak of Israel's future history. Looking back from the 21st century, we can see some amazing parallels. Israel will spend a long period – 'many days' – without a national leader. She will stop using teraphim (household gods) and other forms of idolatry, but shall also do without the blessing of sacrifice to cover sins, and the ephod-wearing high priest to mediate God's will. Think of the last 2000 years since Jesus' blood was shed as the final price of redemption. The Temple was destroyed in AD 70 along with its sacrifices, yet the people of Israel, scattered among the nations, have held to Yahweh their God. He has still loved and protected them – witness the fact that crusades, inquisitions, pogroms, even the Nazi holocaust did not manage to destroy them as a people. But they have not yet experienced the fullness of His love. Verse 5 contains the glorious promise that in the 'last days' they will return home and seek the LORD their God and David their King – a reference to the Messiah. They will be won by His goodness and love back into a full bridal relationship with Him.

 Pray the Word

Praise God for His faithfulness to His people even though He has to judge them! Give thanks that as the Jewish people have returned home to their land over the last two centuries in increasing numbers, there have been an ever-increasing number discovering Jesus their Messiah. Pray for the witness of Messianic Jews today, and for the complete fulfilment of this promise. *'Afterward the children of Israel shall return and seek the LORD their God and David their king. They shall fear the LORD and His goodness in the latter days'* (v5 NKJV).

Think of what it cost Hosea to obey God and pray that you will be willing to love sacrificially. Ask Him to use you as His channel of blessing to Israel, no matter what it costs. *'And may the Lord make you increase and abound in love...'* (1 Thessalonians 3:12).

Pray for those in bondage to prostitution in Israel and throughout the Middle East, and for ministries that seek to reach and help them in Jesus' name. May the Lord grant healing, deliverance and new life through His unconditional love. *'For the LORD has called you like a woman forsaken and grieved in spirit, like a youthful wife, when you were refused, says your God'* (Isaiah 54:6 NKJV).

O LITTLE TOWN OF BETHLEHEM

'But you, O Bethlehem Ephrathah, who are too little to be among the clans of Judah, from you shall come forth for me one who is to be ruler in Israel' (Micah 5:2).

 Passage for study and prayer: Micah 5:1-5

Bethlehem is not a grand place. It is still a small, dusty Middle Eastern town, though it has spread out to enfold outlying villages and several refugee camps. It looks nothing like the sentimental depictions on countless Christmas cards, although thousands of pilgrims still come to take part in the traditional, joyful celebrations of Messiah's birth. Mass Christian emigration to the West in recent decades, often for economic reasons, has meant that this ancient, once overwhelmingly Christian community is now over two thirds Muslim. The economy, always dependent on tourism, has not recovered from its serious decline during the second Palestinian *intifada* (uprising), which also brought the huge, ugly security wall cutting off Bethlehem from Jerusalem. Christians are caught between the opposing sides, suffering the same daily hardships as all Palestinians but also coping with serious discrimination in an increasingly dominant Muslim society. In spite of this, long-established ministries still function effectively and a small community of evangelical believers is alive and growing, and full of hope for revival!

Though small, Bethlehem has always had a prophetic destiny. It featured in the lives of Rachel and Benjamin, Naomi, Ruth the Gentile and Boaz, and above all, Ruth's great-grandson David – the shepherd-king who was born, brought up and called by God in this place. He was the forerunner of the one of whom Micah speaks. Notice that this promised one will come forth from Bethlehem, for God, to be ruler in Israel, as planned from 'ancient days', or from the very beginning.

The birth of Jesus fulfilled this Messianic prophecy, as the angels announced to the shepherds raising the sacrificial lambs for the

Temple in the famous Shepherds Fields. Yet Biblical prophecies often have a double fulfilment. He will come again as Israel's Messiah and King of Kings, so could it be that Bethlehem is still strategic in God's prophetic purposes? Jews are returning to the rest of their brothers in Israel (v3), and the Messiah is their only hope for peace (v5). Most of the believers in the West Bank live in the Bethlehem area and are uniquely placed to be a powerful witness to the Israelis around them, as well as to their Muslim neighbours. Jews are always profoundly affected by genuine Christian love, but how much more when those Christians represent their deadliest enemies? And what spiritual power will be released as Christians forgive and embrace those who hurt or oppress them, and seek to be true peacemakers for Jesus?

 Pray the Word

Pray that the Lord will supply all the spiritual and physical needs of Bethlehem's believers, through His worldwide Body. *'And they shall dwell secure, for now he shall be great to the ends of the earth. And he shall be their peace'* (vv4, 5). May they be true peacemakers no matter what the cost, standing between the opposing sides in the truth, love and power of Jesus.

Pray for Palestinian Christians as they wrestle with scriptures about the restoration of Israel, often very hard for them to accept in terms of their history. *'Therefore he shall give them up until the time when she who is in labour has given birth; then the rest of his brothers shall return to the people of Israel'* (v3). Pray especially for staff and students of the Bethlehem Bible College, a strategic theological ministry training future Christian leaders.

Pray for true revival to come to Bethlehem's churches, anointing and enabling them to fulfil their destiny in the Kingdom of God, especially with regard to the people of Israel. *'And when they had prayed, the place in which they were gathered together was shaken, and they were all filled with the Holy Spirit and continued to speak the word of God with boldness'* (Acts 4:31).

GATHERING CAPTIVES

'They all come for violence, all their faces forward. They gather captives like sand. At kings they scoff, and at rulers they laugh. They laugh at every fortress, for they pile up earth and take it' (Habakkuk 1:9, 10).

 Passage for study and prayer:
Habakkuk 1:1-17

This conversation between the prophet Habakkuk and God gives a vivid picture of the Chaldeans, a warlike people who were rising up in Babylonia under Nebuchadnezzar just as the Assyrian Empire, (centred in Nineveh close to today's northern Iraqi city of Mosul), was on the wane. Chaldea was further south, centred on Babylon about 50 miles from modern Baghdad, and its name lives on in the title of Iraq's largest Christian denomination, the ancient Catholic Chaldean Church. It was a time of chaos and change – much like today, where various Islamist factions have taken advantage of the upheaval caused by the overthrow of previous dictator Saddam Hussein, and the presence of Western troops, to destabilize Iraq and seek to fulfil their own agendas through terrorism. Ordinary Iraqis would no doubt echo Habakkuk's cry for divine intervention and deliverance, as well as answers (vv1-4), as they suffer at the hands of cruel, violent and lawless men, who target the innocent, pursue their own power and are seemingly unstoppable, like the Chaldeans described in verses 7-11.

Their tactics of terror have included suicide attacks and car bombings, death threats and forced evictions from homes; but a favourite one has been kidnapping for ransom or political gain. Since 2003, hundreds of local Iraqi academics, officials and Christians, as well as foreign journalists and contractors, have been held hostage in Iraq. Many have been killed or are still missing. These days Christians, who are often linked in Muslim minds with the 'Christian West', are still frequently bombed or kidnapped – even in the traditional Christian stronghold of the north, where many had previously fled to escape persecution elsewhere. They are seen as a 'soft target' for criminal gangs as well as Islamists, as the local authorities often fail to protect them. Kidnapping has also hugely increased in other nations such as Afghanistan and Yemen; and in Israel, terror groups constantly attempt to abduct soldiers as 'bargaining chips' to obtain political concessions.

The good news is, however, that the Lord is in control! He tells Habakkuk that however hard it is to understand (v5), even such wicked and cruel men can be instruments in His hand (v6), to challenge and reprove His people and extend His Kingdom rule (v12), until He deals with them in His time and way (2:7-12).

 Pray the Word

Cry out to God for Iraq, a country that has suffered so much, and pray that the Lord will fulfil His Kingdom purposes in that nation, and answer the prayers of His people speedily. *'O LORD, how long shall I cry …to you "Violence!" and you will not save?'* (v2). Pray for Christians to be protected and strengthened in their faith, witness and knowledge of God. *'Are you not from everlasting, O LORD my God, my Holy One? We shall not die'* (v12).

Stand in prayer against the evil practice of kidnapping, and pray for supernatural protection for intended victims and the restoration of genuine law and order. *'So the law is paralyzed, and justice never goes forth. For the wicked surround the righteous…'* (v4). Pray for all those held hostage in Iraq, Gaza and other parts of the Middle East, for their protection and speedy release, and for complete physical and emotional healing. *'Even the captives of the mighty shall be taken, and the prey of the tyrant be rescued'* (Isaiah 49:25).

Pray earnestly for those involved in terrorism, to meet the Lord supernaturally and have a total change of heart. Declare God's promise: *'For the earth* [including Iraq!] *will be filled with the knowledge of the glory of the LORD as the waters cover the sea'* (Habakkuk 2:14).

83

'On that day I will seek to destroy all the nations that come against Jerusalem. And I will pour out on the house of David and the inhabitants of Jerusalem a spirit of grace and pleas for mercy, so that, when they look on me, on him whom they have pierced, they shall mourn for him as one mourns for an only son' (Zechariah 12:9, 10).

 **Passage for study and prayer:
Zechariah 12:1-13:2**

Jerusalem and the Jewish people belong together – and Zechariah tells us why. Jerusalem, on that day of reckoning and revelation, is where Israel will finally recognize who Jesus is, and the fountain will be opened that will cleanse them from their sin. In the midst of their fiery trial, as all the nations gather against them, the LORD Himself will keep His eye on them, protecting and strengthening them to fight their enemies (vv4-8). Then, at the moment when their strength is spent, He will open their eyes in an outpouring of grace. As they look to Him – the Hebrew word is much stronger than 'on' or 'at' and implies a forward momentum – they will recognize that the very one whom they had pierced and rejected, is truly the Messiah. Deep repentance follows as the remnant left alive mourn bitterly and cry out for mercy. It will be a very personal response for each individual, as each one grieves in the privacy of his own home (v14). On that day the cleansing fountain of the blood of Jesus will flow to all who will receive it, and those religious leaders who denied Him and taught others to do so will be removed forever, along with all idolatry and spiritual defilement (vv13:1-2).

So that day is a day of reckoning for the people of Israel, but even more so for the nations. The LORD, who created heaven and earth and all mankind, has the right to make Jerusalem a 'cup of staggering' – the image is that of a potent brew causing drunkenness – to the surrounding peoples, as they attack the city and land of the Jews (vv1-2). Or to put it another way, Jerusalem will be a heavy stone and anyone who tries to lift it will gash himself severely (v3). Notice that this second metaphor applies not only to Israel's neighbours, but also to those from every nation who choose to support them. Wherever we live, we have this choice, as the Lord holds Jew and Gentile alike accountable to the revelation of His Word. Today's rising tide of increasingly aggressive world opinion that denies Jewish claims to Jerusalem, is no doubt fuelled by the powers of darkness who seek to prevent the return of the Lord (see chapter 14:4-9). Yet Zechariah says that God Himself is responsible for it. We cannot pray against His purposes, but we can pray for His mercy in judgment and for a huge remnant to receive salvation, not only in Israel but the nations of the world too (Romans 11:15).

 Pray the Word

Pray for God's mercy on your nation, that many in it will choose to stand on His side in the coming battle over Jerusalem. *'On that day I will make Jerusalem a heavy stone for all the peoples. All who lift it will surely hurt themselves'* (v1). Pray especially for many more in the church to be led by the Holy Spirit to intercede for His purposes for Israel. Pray this too for Arab Christians in the Middle East, whose peoples will suffer so greatly in this battle.

Thank God that He will not allow His people and city to be destroyed, and claim in prayer the specific promises in verses 4, 5, 6 and 8, of His supernatural intervention in the coming battle for Jerusalem. *'The inhabitants of Jerusalem have strength through the LORD of hosts, their God'* (v5). Pray that Israelis will trust in Him rather than in their own efforts.

Praise God for the coming mass salvation of the Jewish people and pray that there may be a very large remnant left to receive the gift of repentance and cleansing through the blood of Messiah. *'On that day there shall be a fountain opened for the house of David and the inhabitants of Jerusalem, to cleanse them from sin and uncleanness'* (13:1).

'Now after Jesus was born in Bethlehem of Judea in the days of Herod the king, behold, wise men [magi] from the east came to Jerusalem, saying, "Where is he who has been born king of the Jews? For we saw his star when it rose and have come to worship him"' (Matthew 2:1, 2).

 Passage for study and prayer: Matthew 2:1-12.

This familiar part of the Christmas story has always fascinated Bible students – who were these wise men, and where did they come from? Though the Greek word 'magi' is most often used in the Bible to describe sorcerers and others involved in occult arts, it does not always have a negative meaning. It can simply refer to those with special knowledge and wisdom, like Daniel who became chief of the magi in Babylon (Daniel 4:9). Because 'magi' was the term used for Persian and Chaldean priests, many scholars have assumed they came from Iran or Iraq, but in the Bible, the phrase 'from the east' was never used for those regions, which were reached via the north. Rather, the people of the east were the nomadic tribes inhabiting the Arabian Peninsula and the surrounding deserts, descendants of Abraham through Hagar and Keturah (see for example, Judges 6:33 and Jeremiah 49:28). They controlled the trade in myrrh and frankincense, grown only in southern Arabia, and their gold was famous in the ancient world (Isaiah 60:6).

Is it surprising that the very first Gentiles to worship Jesus as Messiah and King were in fact wealthy and prominent Arabs from the very heart of Arabia? Remember that they were Israel's closest cousins, and before their tribes slid into idolatry just like their Israelite kin, many among them worshipped the true God – for example Jethro the Midianite (Exodus 18:1,12), and Job, 'the greatest of all the people of the East' (Job 1:3). God's promise of blessing to Ishmael and his descendants, and their inheritance close to His covenant people, surely places them at the forefront of His salvation plan for the Gentiles. These wise men certainly knew of the Biblical promise of the Messiah, if not where he would be born (v2). They were not mere casual stargazers, curious about some unusual astrological phenomenon. The star, whether it was an actual astral body or a supernatural manifestation of God's *shekinah* glory, was a sign from the Lord that drew them straight to Jesus (v9). Once there, they responded first with joyful praise (v10) and then extravagant worship (v11), and finally obedience to God's warning through a dream (v12). Their gifts were God's provision for Jesus at a critical time and also prophetically foreshadowed His future ministry. Wise men indeed!

Pray the Word

Praise God for the example of these Arab magi who were open to receive revelation from God, and responded so wholeheartedly. Pray He will give powerful dreams and visions of Jesus to many hungry hearts in Saudi Arabia, Yemen, Bahrain, Kuwait, Oman, Qatar, and the United Arab Emirates, and guide them to true, sacrificial faith in Him. *'We saw… and have come to worship'* (v2).

Pray for expatriate believers working in the Arabian Peninsula in obedience to the call of God, for protection, provision, and effective witness. May they be sustained in the midst of very strong spiritual opposition and warfare, by joyful worship and fellowship with Jesus. *'…they rejoiced exceedingly with great joy… they fell down and worshipped him'* (vv10, 11)

Pray the same for the scattered, mostly secret, local believers. May they grow into mature disciples, freed from the patterns of the Islamic mindset by the power of God's word. *'Do not be conformed to this world, but be transformed by the renewal of your mind'* (Romans 12:2). Pray persistently and in faith for an indigenous church to arise here in the very heartland of Islam, that will be a huge blessing to God's Kingdom.

THE SHEEP AND THE GOATS

'When the Son of Man comes in his glory, and all the angels with him, then he will sit on his glorious throne. Before him will be gathered all the nations, and he will separate people one from another as a shepherd separates the sheep from the goats' (Matthew 25:31, 32).

 Passage for study and prayer: Matthew 25:31-46

Visitors to the Middle East today can still see mixed flocks of sheep and goats grazing together on the hillsides, as his disciples certainly did when Jesus spoke these words to them as part of his 'Olivet Discourse' on the coming Kingdom, shortly before His death. He described His own future return as 'the Son of Man', the King, and how He will judge all the nations, or peoples. He will divide them into two groups, as sheep and goats are separated at the end of the day. The 'sheep' will inherit the Kingdom, on the basis of the love and mercy they showed Him when in need, and the 'goats' will be banished far from God's presence, because they did not show that love and care towards Him. In both cases, the question was asked, 'When did we see you in need?' and in both, the answer was the same: 'When you did it, or did not do it, to the least of these my brethren, you did it or didn't do it to me.' It seems simple enough, yet a closer look raises several important questions.

Feeding the hungry, giving drink to the thirsty, welcoming the stranger, clothing the naked, visiting the sick and seeking out the prisoners are clearly commended as vital expressions of our love for Jesus. By showing compassion, we prove we belong to Him and His Kingdom.

But who are the 'brothers' Jesus is referring to? Some say He means mankind in general, but also, Scripture seems to indicate something more specific. In Matthew 12:49, Jesus calls his followers his brothers and sisters, a point which Paul also makes in teaching that believers are adopted into the family of God (Romans

8:15ff). Without doubt we have a special responsibility to care for fellow-believers who are suffering and in need.

Then, what about Jesus' natural brethren, the Jews? He did not forsake his relationship with his natural family (see e.g. John 7:3, 19:25) or His own people (Matthew 23:37). Paul also greatly loved his 'brothers according to the flesh' – so much, he was willing to give up his own salvation for them (Romans 9:3). Surely we cannot claim Jesus the Jew as our brother and then ignore His natural family when they are in need? If we love Him, we love them – it's as simple as that!

Finally, is Jesus speaking of actual nations, or simply individuals of different nationalities? Though certainly referring to individuals, it may well apply to nations too, as the Bible teaches elsewhere that nations are judged for how they treat His people.

 Pray the Word

Ask Jesus how you can be involved in practically helping the many poor and needy among His Jewish brethren in Israel today. *'Truly, I say to you, as you did it to one of the least of these my brothers, you did it to me'* (v40). Pray for Christian ministries in the Land who are actively fulfilling this calling, and give thanks that many Israelis, used to being hated, are having their ideas about Jesus challenged and changed by Christians who truly love and comfort them.

Pray for needy Arab believers, especially in the Palestinian areas, who often suffer poverty, discrimination and persecution and feel ignored by their world-wide Christian family. Ask the Lord to supply all their needs through His Body. *'As we have opportunity, let us do good to everyone, and especially to those who are of the household of faith'* (Galatians 6:10).

Pray that your nation may be a 'sheep nation', blessed by God for standing with His people Israel, and also with Christians wherever they are in need. *'For the nation and kingdom that will not serve you shall perish; those nations shall be utterly laid waste'* (Isaiah 60:12).

'For I am not ashamed of the gospel, for it is the power of God for salvation to everyone who believes, to the Jew first and also to the Greek' (Romans 1:16).

 Passage for study and prayer: Romans 1:1-20

The first century Roman church consisted of both Jewish and Gentile believers in Jesus and coming from such different backgrounds, they didn't always see eye to eye! Paul's letter to them addresses some important theological questions raised by this mixed assembly. His introduction in these opening verses speaks about the gospel, literally 'good news', which is for all nations (v5). Yet it has a divinely appointed order, to the Jew first, and then the Greek, or Gentile. What does this mean? Does 'first' simply refer to time, as Jews were the first to respond to the preaching of the gospel? Well, they were of course, but this idea of 'to the Jew first', is repeated twice more in chapter 2 – in the context of God's judgment on doing evil (2:9) and His reward for doing good (2:10). These verses clearly do not refer to time. No, Paul is making the larger point that Jews, as members of God's covenant people, already know about Him through the Hebrew Scriptures. They therefore have a priority, an advantage and a greater responsibility than those who were previously outside the covenant and with no knowledge of God. However, Gentiles will also be held accountable in the light of what they know of His divine nature and power through creation (vv18-20).

In this passage, Paul mentions God 12 times, not counting personal pronouns that refer to Him. Jesus by contrast, is mentioned just four times by his name and title, Jesus the Messiah ('anointed one' or Christ), and 3 times as God's Son. Paul is not belittling Jesus in any way, but his first focus in this passage is the covenant-keeping God of Israel. The gospel is God's good news, (v1), about His Son (vv3, 9). It was promised by God in the Hebrew Scriptures (v2), is dependent on His power to save (v16), and reveals His righteousness, or 'covenant saving faithfulness' as it is better understood in Hebraic terms (v17). It came through His Son the Messiah, who was descended in His human lineage from King David as the prophets foretold (v3), but whose resurrection from the dead in the power of the Holy Spirit proved His divine Sonship (v4).

Now Jew and Gentile alike can belong to Jesus, know God's love and be 'set apart' to sanctify His name through their obedience (vv5-7). It is only through their response in faith to the faithfulness of both Father and Son that both Jew and Greek may receive life, as Habakkuk said (v17). Sadly, many Christians focus almost exclusively on Jesus, leading to the common belief that he started a completely new religion that had nothing to do with Israel's God. Nothing could be further from the truth!

 Pray the Word

Praise God for His amazing plan of salvation that unites Jew and Gentile together in the New Covenant of faith! Pray verse 16 for all who proclaim the good news 'to the Jew first', in Israel and the Diaspora, that the Lord will give boldness and anoint the message with power to save.

Pray the same for all those sharing the good news in the Arab world, both with Muslims, and with traditional Christians who may not have a living faith. *'Through [Jesus] we have received grace and apostleship to bring about the obedience of faith for the sake of his name among all the nations'* (v5). Pray for the strengthening of Middle Eastern believers, whether at home or abroad.

Give thanks for the insights coming afresh into the church as Jewish and Gentile scholars study God's Word together from the same Hebraic perspective as Jesus and Paul. Pray for Hebraic understanding to penetrate traditional Greek-influenced theology so that Christians everywhere may be strengthened to walk in truly Biblical faith. *'For I long to … impart to you some spiritual gift to strengthen you, that we may be mutually encouraged by each other's faith'* (vv11, 12).

'See to it that no one takes you captive by philosophy and empty deceit, according to human tradition, according to the elemental spirits of the world, and not according to Christ' (Colossians 2:8).

 Passage for study and prayer: Colossians 2:1-23

When Paul wrote this letter to the Colossians, the entire religious world of the time was rife with ideas and philosophies that centred on esoteric knowledge (*gnosis* in Greek); secret mysteries that would lead those who were 'in the know' to spiritual truth or experiences hidden from lesser mortals. Most derived from the ancient mystery religions of Babylon and Egypt, based on occult idol worship. Paul however makes it quite clear that for God's people, the knowledge of His mystery is actually and totally centred in the Messiah (v2). In Him are hidden all the treasures of wisdom and knowledge (v3).

We can be led astray by intellectual arguments, deceitful philosophies, and human traditions which actually originate from demonic spirits (v8). However, in Jesus we see embodied all we need to know of God (v9). As we share in all that he is and has accomplished through the cross, we have real power to live a holy life (vv11-15). Mere religious regulations or unbiblical supernatural experiences may seem to be spiritual, but they have no power to deliver us from sin or bring us to maturity in Messiah (vv16-23).

If it is only through the Messiah that God's mystery can be known, is it surprising that those who reject Him are prey to demonic deception? Many Jews and even some Gentiles today follow the teachings and practice of Kabbalah. Literally meaning 'to receive', Kabbalah is a rabbinic mysticism that has its roots amongst the Gnostic philosophies of Paul's time, though it was further developed in the Middle Ages. Teaching that there are hidden meanings in Scripture that have been revealed to a favoured few, this tradition is passed down from master to disciple to enable its followers to reach self-perfection and union with God. It purports to reveal the 'soul' of Torah, as opposed to its 'body' which is the written Bible, but Kabbalah is in fact man-centred, occult, and opposed to orthodox biblical doctrine. Sadly, many embrace it because they are hungry for God, but end up taken captive by 'elemental spirits'. It is very difficult to break free. Spiritual leaders are seen as the channel of salvation, and exercise great power over their disciples. Not all religious Jews follow Kabbalah, and it takes various forms within different streams of Judaism. However, it always brings deep spiritual darkness by denying the plain meaning of Scripture and the truth about the Messiah.

 Pray the Word

Praise God that Jesus has overcome all demonic powers through His death and resurrection! *'He disarmed the rulers and authorities and put them to open shame, by triumphing over them in him'* (v15). Pray for strong spiritual warriors to fight faithfully in prayer for those held captive by Kabbalah. *'For I want you to know how great a struggle I have for you ... to reach all the riches of full assurance of understanding and the knowledge of God's mystery, which is Christ* (vv1, 2).

Pray for those in various ultra-orthodox sects whose lives are dominated by these traditions, to become aware of their emptiness and lack of real answers to life's problems: *'These have indeed an appearance of wisdom in promoting self-made religion and asceticism and severity to the body, but they are of no value in stopping the indulgence of the flesh'* (v23). Pray they will seek and find the Messiah, *'in whom are hidden all the treasures of wisdom and knowledge* (v3).

Pray for those who have come to faith in Jesus to be completely set free from their rabbis, their community, and their previous ways of thinking: *'Therefore, as you received Christ Jesus the Lord, so walk in him'* (v6). Proclaim this whole passage over those Messianic Jews in danger of being deceived and drawn away from the truth by any teaching or practice of rabbinic Judaism that is unscriptural.

ORDER RESOURCES

The 40 day format of the **Praying God's Word** series lends itself to personal reflection and prayer – especially at Lent. The prayer ideas are also a helpful prompt for small group prayer with the Bible reading and reflection helping people pray with insight.

You can obtain more for use in your church or small group in 3 ways:

- Via your local Christian bookshop
- Via www.amazon.co.uk
- By ordering from *Praying God's Word*

Three resources are available at this time.

Praying for the Peace of Jerusalem
Helping you pray with biblical insight into God's agenda for Israel today.

Penny Valentine   Tahilla Press   ISBN 978-1-84291-187-2

Praying for Israel and the Arab Nations
Further biblical prayer for Israel and for God's salvation purposes for the surrounding nations.

Penny Valentine   Tahilla Press   ISBN 978-1-907228-07-0

Praying the Foundations of the Kingdom of God
Drawing insights from the Torah, the first 5 books of the Old Testament, this 40 part practical study will help you pray in ways that reflect the character of God.

If ordering from *Praying God's Word* please note the following:

- Books are priced at £6 each
- Postage is an additional £1.50 (1-2 copies), £1 per book for 3 or more copies

- Make cheques or postal orders payable to *Praying God's Word*
- Write stating quantities and name(s) of books required to: Praying God's Word, The Old Chapel, Twitchen Clunbury Craven Arms, Shropshire, SY7 0HN United Kingdom